International Perspectives on Yanagita Kunio and Japanese Folklore Studies

Edited by
J. Victor Koschmann,
Ōiwa Keibō and Yamashita Shinji

T0335253

East Asia Program
Cornell University
Ithaca, New York 14853

The *Cornell East Asia Series* publishes manuscripts on a wide variety of scholarly topics pertaining to East Asia. Manuscripts are published on the basis of camera-ready copy provided by the volume author or editor.

Inquiries should be addressed to Editorial Board, Cornell East Asia Series, East Asia Program, Cornell University, 140 Uris Hall, Ithaca, New York 14853.

Third printing 1993
ISSN 1050-2955
ISBN 0-939657-37-6

TABLE OF CONTENTS

PREFACE

This volume has its origins in a study group among the editors at Cornell University. Almost as soon as we had met, in the fall of 1981, we selected some texts by and about the Japanese folklorist Yanagita Kunio (1875-1962) and started meeting every Friday afternoon for discussion. We each arrived at an interest in Yanagita from a different direction.

Yamashita Shinji, a Japanese anthropologist who has done field work in Indonesia, explained that "Yanagita is coming back to me." He felt that Yanagita, whose work he had read as an undergraduate student, had become increasingly relevant again as Yamashita's own concern with the society and culture of his native Japan increased. He also had a theoretical interest in reassessing Yanagita's achievement from the viewpoint of modern anthropology.

Victor Koschmann, a specialist in Japanese intellectual history, seems to have shared with many contemporary Japanese the impression that Yanagita's work stands as one of the most interesting intellectual and cultural phenomena of Japan's modern history.

As for me, after a period of alienating myself from the "Yanagita boom" in Japan, I slowly realized that Yanagita and his thought had begun to function as a convenient "model" in the context of my own study. First, as a group of leading Japanese thinkers have shown in their research on tenkō (intellectual conversion),[1] Yanagita's position, which may be called a progressive conservatism, seemed to present itself as a unique example of intransigent resistance against

---

1. The so-called postwar tenkō research, organized by a group of Japanese intellectuals, was a comparative study of intellectual case histories. Its special focus was on the moments of redirection in thought, or tenkō, vis-à-vis the socio-political oppression of prewar and wartime Japan.

the severe oppression of thought and expression that occurred in war-time Japan. Secondly, as I moved toward the discipline of anthropology, I came to see in Yanagita a suggestive model for anthropological thought. It seemed to me that his definition of folklore, as the self-reflections of ordinary people, did not necessarily imply that the foreign anthropologist had to be replaced by a native, but did succeed in raising the fundamental point that an understanding of oneself and one's own culture must underlie an understanding of others. This point had been brought home to me the previous summer as I read Drylongso by the Black American anthropologist John Gwaltney. In fact, I caught myself superimposing the "Yanagita model" over his idea of "native anthropology."

Who can assert that we ourselves were not influenced by Japan's "Yanagita boom," in which the scholar had been enshrined as a cultural hero by intellectuals, publishers, and a wide range of readers? Yet it seemed possible to hope that our vantage point--on this side of the Pacific--would help us to view Yanagita and his popularity in a relatively detached, objective manner. We began to doubt that his popularity was attributable solely to peculiarities in the contemporary Japanese situation; and we found unsatisfying the view that Yanagita, as a Japanese cultural phenomenon, was thus "untranslatable" into any other context.

By October 1981 we had decided to organize a workshop, taking advantage of the temporary presence in Montreal of two distinguished Yanagita scholars, Tada Michitarō and Yoneyama Toshinao. As we aired our plans more widely, however, it soon became clear that many in the field of Japanese studies were much more interested in the "Yanagita boom" than in Yanagita and his works. That might have been because the great bulk of Yanagita's writing is still untranslated, and hardly mentioned in foreign languages. It thus has remained unknown even to those who often hear Japanese references to it. At the same time, one could not help wondering if it would be worthwhile to spend the great time and effort translating Yanagita's work when many

vi

seemed already to have passed judgment on it: "it's very Japanese," they would say with a smile. Could Yanagita be at all meaningful when detached from the Japanese context?

In order to deal with these questions, we wanted to take into account constructively even the indifferent, or sometimes quite critical, attitudes that were expressed toward Yanagita, because they seemed to indicate the possibility of a fresh point of view. We also hoped they would help us to reconsider critically what Japanese readers had been taking for granted.

Many concluded that Yanagita's writing had gained such acclaim in Japan because of its literary and poetic qualities, rather than for any social-scientific value. An essay by Tsurumi Kazuko,[2] in which she argues that Yanagita's works can make a unique academic contribution in the international community of social science, was greeted with skepticism by many graduate students in anthropology. Even those who had already done some research on his work were often interested only analyzing Yanagita's position into its theoretical elements, identifying equivalents in Western scholarly works, and assessing his place in social science accordingly.

As we proceeded with planning and preparation for the workshop my own frustration grew. Even as I strove to appreciate the detached, "unfriendly" view toward Yanagita, I found myself becoming more and more involved in his works. They were enjoyable, and often exciting. But that could not be enough. I did not want to agree with those who consigned Yanagita entirely to the realm of literature. I wanted badly to express objectively--"academically," if necessary--the sources of my excitement; that had to be the only way a "translation" of Yanagita from one context to another might be possible. In the first draft of our proposal, Yamashita had asked, "Can Yanagita cross the border?" He might have been feeling the same

---

2. Tsurumi Kazuko, "Shakai hendō no paradaimu--Yanagita Kunio no shigoto o jiku to shite," in Tsurumi Kazuko and Ichii Saburō, eds., Shisō no bōken (Tokyo: Chikuma Shobō, 1974).

frustration. Thus, when we decided, after some hesitation, to en-
title the workshop "Yanagita Kunio in International Perspective" we
took a certain risk.

When I traveled to Montreal for a preliminary meeting, I told
the Japanese professors, Tada and Yoneyama, that we hoped the workshop would "dislocate" the so-called Yanagita boom, and test those
Japanese intellectuals who had invented such terms as "Yanagita-
gaku," or Yanagita Studies. Only one thing would be prohibited, I
added, half-seriously: no one would be allowed to say that the subtle
joy of Yanagita could be appreciated only by native Japanese! No
doubt, such a caveat was entirely unnecessary for scholars who had
braved the Montreal winter for the sole purpose of conveying aspects
of Japanese culture to non-Japanese students in their own languages.
Surely, I thought, when that energy was extended to a consideration
of Yanagita, whose great influence on them they acknowledged, their
participation would in itself be a significant event.

Gradually, plans were made and the structure of the coming
workshop became clearer. Our second priority, next to making possible the participation of the Japanese professors, was to introduce
some work that had been done on Yanagita by non-Japanese scholars.
The third was to organize a discussion around Yanagita's About Our
Ancestors (English translation of Senzo no hanashi), that could en-
gage people with various backgrounds who might never have heard of
Yanagita.

* * * * * *

This volume is an incomplete collection of papers given in the
course of the Yanagita workshop. Most remain substantially in their
original form, although in some cases they were subsequently revised
or expanded. Koschmann's paper was written after the workshop, and
Steve Nussbaum's annotated translation in Part III was also added
later. It is unfortunate that we could not include a transcript of

the arguments and discussions that filled the time between papers, and after hours. We are glad, however, that we are able to share a major portion of the contents of that interaction with a broader audience.

We would like to thank all participants for their contributions, large or small. We are particularly appreciative of the major efforts of three whose comments are not included here: S. Robert Ramsey, Assistant Professor of East Asian Languages and Cultures at Columbia University, made a presentation based on the contents of a recent article in the Journal of Japanese Studies;[3] Robert J. Smith, Goldwin Smith Professor of Anthropology at Cornell University, chaired the panel on About Our Ancestors; James A. Boon, Professor of Anthropology at Cornell, acted as respondent to that panel. We are also grateful to many friends in both Ithaca and Montreal, especially Katō Norihiro and Stephen Nussbaum, whose help and suggestions were essential, and Kazuko Smith for her calligraphy. Finally, we are most thankful to the China-Japan Program of Cornell University for sponsoring the event in its entirety.

Ōiwa Keibō
Montreal, July 1983

NOTE: Japanese names follow the convention of surname first.

---

3. S. Robert Ramsey, "Language Change in Japan and the Odyssey of a Teisetsu," Journal of Japanese Studies, Winter 1982.

INTRODUCTION

J. Victor Koschmann

The papers in Part I provide an overview of Yanagita's work, life, and broad appeal to post-World War II Japanese intellectuals. They also touch on many of the themes that are given more detailed treatment in other papers, such as the Yanagita style, the methodology of his discipline of Minzokugaku (Japanese Folklore Studies), his relation to nationalism, and place in the modern Japanese intellectual tradition. Contributions in Part II focus on particular problems or aspects of Yanagita's work, while Part III provides a sample in translation of Yanagita's writing. The selection in Part III also serves as source material for several of the papers.

Since every essay deals with some aspect of Yanagita's life or work, this collection of papers has a certain natural unity. Yet the image of Yanagita that emerges is a somewhat fractured one. His work is viewed variously as a key factor in the process of nation-building, a protest against the academic and administrative establishments, an important contribution to Japanese Literature, an ideological and emotional lodestone for later Japanese intellectuals, a dogmatic "theology," and an "unscientific science" devoted to the evocation of quotidian experience.

Needless to say, such a diversity of viewpoint entails a certain degree of friction. Since the papers themselves leave this potential for conflict largely implicit, I will attempt in this introduction to coax into clearer view two of this collection's major controversies. The first has to do with the degree of validity that can be attributed to Yanagita's work on methodological grounds. It therefore involves the way science is defined and the degree to which a scientific approach should be considered normative. The second is

1

substantive rather than methodological, and relates to the political significance of Yanagita's work. Was it basically on the side of the prewar state and its surrounding establishment, or opposed to it in some manner, or perhaps both?

As suggested in the Preface, problems of method were central to the original impetus behind the Workshop that produced the papers. Moreover, a methodological focus was built in to the discussion from the beginning, when Bernard Bernier was asked to consider Yanagita's About Our Ancestors from a social scientific point of view. Other papers touched on the theme as well, and as a result it emerged as a center of critical attention.

Bernier does not insist that social science provides the only legitimate or potentially fruitful perspective from which to view Yanagita's works; nor does he claim that About Our Ancestors is necessarily representative of Yanagita's work as a whole, although he generally proceeds on that assumption. Nevertheless, his conclusions are provocative: Yanagita's approach is not only unscientific but "theological" because, first, of its attempt to support predetermined conclusions based on "faith" rather than a more empirical commitment to the processes of comprehension and explanation; second, because of its "unhistorical" supposition that existing social and religious patterns are the result of degeneration from a "pristine state" in the past, and third, because of its assumption of Japan's "total uniqueness." These charges mount a direct challenge to those who find in Yanagita's mode of collecting and interpreting popular lore a valid means of apprehending social reality.

The contribution by Tada Michitarō provides an equally provocative and bold statement of an opposing view. Tada characterizes Yanagita's method in various ways: as abduction as opposed to deduction or induction, as an "evocation" of experience, and as a situational understanding of behavior. Moreover, he argues that as a way of approaching social reality it is clearly superior to social-scientific reasoning, which he criticizes as "the imposition of a concept on a phenomenon." He clearly prefers what he believes to be Yanagita's ironically "unscientific science," whose practitioners discern by participating, and help to create the object of research even as they observe it. How close this procedure is to what Bernier calls comprehension (in contrast to explanation) is uncertain, but it is unlikely that Tada could ever accept Bernier's charge that Yanagita's accounts of social reality are premised upon the prejudgment of "faith."

Tada's celebration of the methodological paradox latent in Yanagita's "unscientific science" is mirrored in his own style of presentation. Oscillating between statements about Yanagita and "imitations" of him, Tada's narrative itself represents an ironic tension between objective commentary and subjective involvement, and between the description of action and action itself. Apparently, whereas Bernier believes that Yanagita's lack of objectivity has to be analyzed objectively, Tada insists that Yanagita's method of subjective involvement can only properly be understood through imitative participation.

One basis for this methodological confrontation is, no doubt, to be found in Yanagita's own work, as interpreted in these and other papers. Yamashita describes Yanagita's belief that, in Japanese religion, objective distinctions between the living and the dead, worshipper and ancestor, are reduced to a unifying process of "being with," "playing," or "living," that is immediate and undifferentiated. He also discusses Yanagita's search for a tradition that is unconscious and thus nonverbal, preserved in behavior rather than written down (see the translation in Part III). Here too, the mediacy implied by writing, consciousness, and spacio-temporal distance is replaced by the immediacy of unconscious, active "being."

Ōiwa highlights Yanagita's tendency to move by means of etymological or dialectological reductions from an objectively analytical form of language to a "core" of pure activity; that is, his desire to capture through language itself a prelinguistic "moment of life."

This emphasis on inner vitality is paralleled in the construction of Yanagita's "science" of Japanese Folklore Studies, which was designed specifically to by-pass writing--thought to be the most objectified and "dead" form of language--and to concentrate rather on the "living," verbal past that lay hidden in everyday social life.

It is Yanagita's urge to penetrate beyond modern objectivity and alienation in order to reach a realm of self-identity that seems to cause such radical divisions among his readers. For Bernier, this quest amounts to seeking "'total participation' with another person or reality" (82), and leads, along with "dogmatism," to "theological" claims of absolute truth. For Tada, on the other hand, it is a valid goal which can be attained only through an open, empathetic posture of abduction: "In tradition and ritual true feelings are hidden; they lie in the shadow and are indiscernible and unknown to anyone unless that person places himself in a situation where he can share such an experience" (98).

Etymologies provide an interesting case in point. For Yamashita, Yanagita's etymological excursions function to "'revitalize' the authentic power of a word which over time has sunk into the deep, unconscious strata of people's minds" (61). Here, the accuracy of the procedure is less important than its function. A similar view seems to be held by Tada, whose own imitation of Yanagita is rich in etymological reductions, which not only provide insight but lead to ironic reversals of conventional assumptions. For Bernier, however, along with such insights will inevitably come "arbitrary and conjectural conclusions," and they should therefore be viewed with skepticism (79).

Ōiwa suggests that Yanagita's etymologies most often lead away from the objective surface of language to a deeper level where nouns become verbs and one encounters the "unobjectified aspect of language," or a root concept that represents "an archetype of human action" (129). He explicitly connects Yanagita's frequent use of etymology to similar reductive strategies employed by Motoori

Norinaga (1730-1801) and others in the early-modern tradition of
Kokugaku, or nativism. As Harry Harootunian has shown, Motoori
sought to rediscover an archaic level of pure metaphor which preceded
Chinese influence.[1] A major difference between Motoori and Yanagita,
of course, was that while the former had no choice but to use written
texts as the medium through which to discover original immediacy, the
latter discovered an alternative in the semiologically differentiated
texture of local society.

Ōiwa also points to Yanagita's criticism of "language worship,"
and his implicit preference, not only for verbal language over writing, but for nonverbal expression (wailing, dancing) over the verbal.
Presumably, the next step in this reductive direction could only be
silence: the "unconscious" ritual performance highlighted by Yamashita, or even the clownish hyottoko mask, which according to Tada
represents the native Japanese deity, Kunitsukami, who is unable to
reply to the foreign, "scientific" deity Amatsukami. The Amatsu-
kami/Kunitsukami model is suggestive in other ways as well. If we
equate Amatsukami with the urban, elite ethnologist and Kunitsukami
with the rural, common folk (jōmin) whom the ethnologist attempts to
study, we are more apt to understand why Yanagita thought that ulti-
mately the inner life of village people could only be grasped
"introspectively" by the villagers themselves. When queried from
outside, the villagers are silent, "inaudible" in a way that reminds
us of Tsurumi Kazuko's description of the "invisible" history of
Japanese villagers, whose lack of writing made them inaccessible to
conventional historiographical method (158-59).

Tada would claim, presumably, that Yanagita's approach is capable of penetrating the silence and invisibility of this common
stratum of Japanese society, while the conceptual framework employed
by Bernier and other outsiders would be answered only by the mask of

---

1. H. D. Harootunian, "The Consciousness of Archaic Form in
the New Realism of Kokugaku," in Najita Tetsuo and Irwin Scheiner,
eds., Japanese Thought in the Tokugawa Period (Chicago: University of
Chicago Press, 1978).

the _hyottoko_. Bernier, on the other hand, appears to feel that the villagers of Sone, where he carried out his field work, responded to his queries quite adequately. It is apparent that the different views of Yanagita's method that are revealed in these papers are closely connected to the predispositions of their authors, and are still far from resolved.

The question of Yanagita's relation to nationalism and the prewar state was not as controversial as methodology at the Workshop itself, perhaps because the Koschmann paper, which focuses entirely on resistance against the establishment, was not completed at the time. Nevertheless several of the papers touch on aspects of this question, and it might be useful to draw together the various viewpoints expressed.

Yoneyama defines Yanagita's discipline of Minzokugaku as a "Volkskunde für Japanischen," intended as the study of Japanese by Japanese. The nationalistic overtones are clear, and Yoneyama calls attention to them further by drawing a parallel with African movements that seek to create a national identity out of diverse cultural and linguistic components. Whereas the Meiji government imposed from the center such symbols as the emperor, Constitution, and civil codes, Yanagita sought to orient a national culture around the local traditions and folk believes that were in danger of being overwhelmed by state nationalism. Thus, Yoneyama sees Yanagita as contributing to nationalism, but a nationalism "from the bottom up" rather than from the top down.

Bernier takes a more extreme position, placing Yanagita's views with respect to kinship and cultural uniqueness on the side of the official prewar ideology of the "family state" and the unbroken imperial line (_kokutai_). Indeed, Bernier finds Yanagita's "emotional appeal" to intellectuals potentially dangerous and prefers to draw a parallel not to contemporary processes of "nation building" but rather to the support of German intellectuals for Nazism.

Ronald Morse acknowledges the sometimes "nationalistic" impact of Yanagita's early work, The Legends of Tōno (translated by Morse). Yet he also suggests that the work should be viewed in the context of modern Japanese literature, particularly Meiji "naturalism," and that for Yanagita, as for other creative writers of the time, such works offered channels for the redirection of urges toward social protest and revolution. Certainly, as Tsurumi Kazuko has also pointed out (144), the Tōno tales are replete with anecdotes that contravene schoolroom ethics and the officially-sponsored morality of the "emperor system."

Koschmann's paper attempts to deal systematically with the question of political significance, largely by introducing the arguments made by post-World War II Japanese intellectuals who see in Yanagita's work a trajectory of resistance against the "emperor system." Their occasional suggestion--on the basis of a few incidents such as his petitioning activity against shrine consolidation--that Yanagita intentionally confronted the state are not very convincing guides to the overall political significance of his work. Some of Yanagita's early studies did deal with such marginal groups as the mountain dwellers and wanderers, whom elite culture tended to ignore, and some of his theories had the subversive implication of reversing that marginality. Probably most important, however, is their perception, which is extended and amplified in the paper, that the discipline of Folklore Studies itself, as it was constituted by Yanagita in the mid-1930s, functioned as a "counter-discipline" (Tada uses the term "counter-consciousness") which tended to contravene the tenets of scholarship and the definition of truth upon which the modern Japanese establishment relied. The ultimate effect of such an argument, however, is to shift attention away from the question of the political stance specific to Folklore Studies toward the problem of how scholarship and the state were linked, structurally and over time, in the first forty-odd years of the twentieth century. Although Foucault's notion of a "regime of truth" is suggestive, more work is required in order to substantiate its applicability to prewar Japan.

Partial and disparate though they are, therefore, the essays included here not only illuminate some important aspects of Yanagita's work. They also point beyond Yanagita to a number of broader issues: the nature and significance of nationalism, the boundaries among literature, intellectual history and social science, the appropriate stance of the researcher in relation to the culture he or she sets out to study, the role of linguistics in culture and social research, and the forms of intellectual and political domination exercised in modern Japan. I hope we have succeeded in demonstrating that Yanagita's work offers a fruitful point of reference for the exploration of these and other major issues, and that others will take up the challenge presented by his voluminous work.

PART I

YANAGITA KUNIO AND HIS APPEAL

YANAGITA KUNIO, AND THE MODERN JAPANESE CONSCIOUSNESS

Ronald A. Morse

When I was asked to speak about Yanagita Kunio (July 31, 1875-August 8, 1962) my first instinct was to focus in narrowly and discuss what I knew best--the book I translated in 1975 by Yanagita, The Legends of Tōno (1910). Upon reflection I realized that this might not be the most appropriate topic for a group of people who had no prior knowledge about Yanagita Kunio and were unfamiliar with the nature of his studies.

When I was asked about a title, I decided to broaden the scope of my comments. Experience has taught me that folklore is certainly something worthy of examination, but as a topic for a lecture it fired up little interest. It also seemed that I had a responsibility to explain how Yanagita, despite the remote and unique nature of his writings, got to be such a popular figure in recent times in Japan. The word "counter-culture"--the jargon of the 1970s for anti-establishment attitudes and behavior--also seemed appropriate for discussing Yanagita. Yanagita has been a hero for anti-establishment groups in Japan.

Finally, it seemed to me that the modern Japanese aesthetic consciousness had something to do with why people were interested in Yanagita Kunio.[1] As you can imagine by now, I linked all three ideas for this lecture. What I would like to share with you is a very personal analysis of how folklore studies, which is really "Yanagita studies" in Japan, was formed, how the postwar world of Japanese

---

1. See my unpublished dissertation The Search for Japan's National Character and Distinctiveness: Yanagita Kunio (1875-1962) and the Folklore Movement (1974). This appeared in Japanese as Kindaika e no chosen (1977).

intellectualism turned to this "nativistic" thinker for inspiration and how Yanagita, by speaking to very basic humanistic needs, has helped modern Japan formulate a sensibility to cope with change in the modern world. Here I use the term "humanistic," not in the elite sense, but in the folklore sense--the culture of the non-elite. Folklore broadens the traditional concept of the humanities in three ways: it elucidates the tension between tradition and creativity, it emphasizes the oral (expressive) culture and it stretches mental horizons through the appreciation of cultural diversity.[2]

Many people interested in Yanagita, the man, have characterized him as the dean of Japanese folklore studies and as someone occupying a special position in Japanese intellectual history. They have suggested that he founded a unique discipline sometimes called "the study of the common man" and that there are important lessons to be derived about Japanese culture and history from his writings. This is exactly what I thought a decade ago as I left Princeton for Japan to complete my research on Yanagita and the establishment of folklore studies in Japan. I had been in Japan in the late 1960s when Yanagita was "high fashion"--everyone from housewives nostalgic for rural folkcraft items for their homes to Marxist intellectuals searching for an indigenous critique of the elite-capitalist exploitation of Japan (and even business executives anxious for some meaningful explanation of how they survived each boring day) felt that Yanagita's writings could speak to their yearnings for meaning in wake of the rushed, materialistic, post-war prosperity. Folklore, interpreted as an echo of the past and a vigorous voice of the present, spoke to the rising tide of nostalgia about the sources of Japan's past. New theories about Japanese society seemed to be invented monthly and Yanagita offered a vast repository of interesting ideas on almost every aspect of Japanese culture. There was hardly a subject he hadn't covered in his 88 years. Yanagita's collected works (36

---

2. See Richard M. Dorson, "The Value of the Humanities: A Folklorist's View," in Humanist as Citizen, edited by John Agresto and Peter Reisenberg.

volumes) sold over 60,000 sets in the 1970s. The secondary literature about him is also voluminous.

Japanese society was reflecting upon itself in new ways at this
time. The dialogue between Western civilization and Japanese culture
that had so preoccupied Meiji enlightenment scholars was once again
placed at the center of Japanese intellectual life. With American
attitudes and institutions guiding the reform of Japan it was to be
only a matter of time before the Japanese would begin to seek out and
emphasize those aspects of the Japanese tradition that seemed to
endure. Intellectuals, as is their role, responded most acutely to
all of these tensions. They felt they had to respond to the felt
unreliability of human experience brought about by what seemed the
inhuman acceleration of historical change. As Susan Sontag, speaking
in a much broader context said:

> Most serious thought in our time struggles with the
> feeling of homelessness. The felt unreliability of
> human experience that brought about the inhuman
> acceleration of historical change has led every
> sensitive modern mind to the recording of some kind
> of nausea, of intellectual vertigo.[3]

Japanese in general, largely because of their receptivity to
foreign cultures and the U.S. occupation of Japan in 1945, feel a
homelessness that we in the United States have not suffered, at least
not in the same way. Yanagita for many reasons became "Cultural
Fashion"--he was the "celebrity" intellectual of the 1970s. It was
in this gush of nostalgia for Japan's past that I enthusiastically
translated Yanagita's finest work, The Legends of Tōno, and completed
my dissertation. Having experienced the student movement of the '60s
at Berkeley, I understand the fear of a "one-dimensional man," and
lived through, with many, the damage done to our society by the Viet-
nam War. I felt that I could empathize with and understand the

---

3. "The Anthropologist as Hero," in E. N. Hayes and T. Hayes
(eds.) Claude Levi-Strauss: The Anthropologist as Hero (1970), p.
185.

feelings of those using Yanagita to critique their society and get a grip on their own lives.

Many scholars have written about the tensions, both past and present, in the Japanese psyche between traditional elements and modern (foreign) introductions. Usually these forces are in conflict --sometimes consciously, sometimes unconsciously--the resolution of the tension being some kind of indigenous intellectual synthesis that will make sense out of the world. Some critics doubt this synthesis can take place. As Tsurumi Kazuko has stated, the Japanese mind does not strive for integration and synthesis but is comfortable with a dresser drawer type of construction in which each ideology or belief is comfortably stored away, always available when needed. Each ideology is given its own independent existence. Tsurumi, who finds this to be true of Yanagita's approach, points to one of the difficulties in using Yanagita's works to conduct research on Japan.

Now, a decade later and a good eight years since the Yanagita boom ended, I have been asked to comment on this "folklore giant" who is seen as important in modern Japanese intellectual history. My earlier enthusiasm for Yanagita has now waned. My hope to educate America by the example of Yanagita and Japan and my hope for Japan to transform itself by Yanagita's measure have gone the way of most such notions. The barrenness of modern Japanese intellectual history seems more evident today as I reflect back on the flow of Japan's modern development. Perhaps this is because of changes more in my thinking than in those regarding Yanagita? More questions than answers seem to come to mind. Why was there no intellectual resistance in Japan during World War II? Why do Japanese thought and writing seem empty and superficial when read in the original or even in translations? What idea or principle has Japan contributed to the world in the postwar era? Are there common universal standards against which Japan can be tested? Has our cultural ethnocentrism blocked us from fully appreciating Japan's contributions? How does one make sense out of such a different tradition? Ezra Vogel, in his recent book, Japan as Number 1, gives us no answers to these deeper philosophical questions.

I am not sure there are answers to these questions, but by examining Yanagita's career up to the time he wrote The Legends of Tōno, I would like to explore the issues Yanagita personally faced and try to relate those issues to the broader questions about more recent Japanese history.

"The Legends of Tono" as History

It is just twenty years since Yanagita passed away, and a variety of groups in Japan are using the occasion to re-examine issues of Japanese society and explore how Yanagita dealt with them. Yanagita had a career which never pointed in a single direction--he got started as a poet and writer, was a government official for twenty years, became a journalist in 1920, formed the first folklore groups, and survived World War II to become something of a symbol for a democratic Japan because of his writings and attention to Japanese non-elite, cultural traditions and thought. Yanagita was something of a dandy in his early days (around 1900-1910 when he wrote The Legends of Tōno); he disagreed with Meiji policies on rural reform and left the government in despair to be a journalist. He wrote About Our Ancestors (1945) during a conservative, religious phase, during the dark days of World War II, when he feared for the survival of his family line. Yanagita never had doubts about the creativity and genius of the Japanese people. He was for reform and change as long as it was done in a meaningful way, by which he meant in line with the finer and more sensible qualities of the Japanese common man. His writings, not academic or packed with data, were intended to stimulate interest in the Japanese tradition and motivate individual readers to take an interest in their own culture. His earlier writings were more detailed and literary, but all of his works were compiled with an educational and sensitizing function.

I would like to focus on The Legends of Tōno for two reasons. The work is important because it stands between literature and politics, the two elements that guided Yanagita's career. The book is also important, and I will soon turn to this in greater detail, because it indicates the guiding principles of Yanagita's career. The Legends of Tōno is genuinely Japanese and consciously literary. This explains its appeal and enduring significance. The other reason for looking at The Legends of Tōno is because of the tremendous literary impact the book has had in Japan, especially among the thinkers and men of culture, but even more broadly among the literate elite of Japan. From 1910, when the Legends appeared, down to the present, Japanese have been deeply moved by the style and content of The Legends of Tōno. Let me give you just two recent examples of how the work has fired the minds of those seeking to grasp the essence of Japan's modern transformation.

(1) Yoshimoto Takaaki (Ryūmei), a gifted poet and critic, began studying literature in the late 1930s. Frustrated over the failure of his efforts with the Communist League during the Security Treaty struggle (1960), he tried to reach beyond sectarian radicalism by exploring the aesthetics of Japanese language and poetry. In 1969, when he published Kyōdō gensōron (The Psychic World of Shared Fantasies), he used a Freudian approach to the questions of the psychic structures revealed in Japanese literature. This book, which appealed to the growing experience-oriented, anti-intellectualism of students in the late 1960s, compared episodes in the 8th-century Kojiki with stories from The Legends of Tōno. Yoshimoto's cultural aestheticism is not radically different from the style of another modern writer and novelist, Mishima Yukio. Mishima, in one of his last works (What Is a Novel?), placed folklore alongside psychoanalysis and materialism as one approach in examining the Japanese collective will. The folklore method as developed by Yanagita, he maintained, utilized external forms to explore beauty and inner emotion. Mishima read Yoshimoto's Kyōdō gensōron, and detected a new relationship between Japanese classical literature and the oral

folklore tradition. Mishima saw death, as portrayed in Tono monogatari, as suggesting a new method for the analysis of Japan.

(2) To take one more example, the attitudes of Kyōto University professors on Yanagita are reflected in the careers of Katō
Hidetoshi (1930-), a sociologist, and Yoneyama Toshinao (1930-), an
anthropologist. Kyōto University scholars have serious reservations
about Yanagita's approach, yet they recognize that there are important aspects of folklore research which can be of use in their own
research. In 1963 when Katō and Yoneyama did a cultural survey of
the area in Iwate Prefecture that included Tōno City, they wrote that
it was Yanagita's Tōno monogatari that made them conscious of the
need to evaluate Japan by Japanese not foreign standards. Their own
training in American social science methods had, they reflected,
turned them into foreigners evaluating Japan by foreign criteria.
This feeling that foreign social science models and theories are of
limited usefulness in understanding Asian late-developing nations was
shared by many Japanese.

Protest in Japan has seldom led to revolution; it is usually
turned inward and expressed in a literary form of culturalism much
like Yanagita's work. If true revolution seems impossible in Japan
and literature serves as the escape valve for Japanese protest--the
vehicle through which the inner need to rebel is expressed as an
alternative to social action--then it is important to grasp the
literary qualities of The Legends of Tōno to understand its appeal to
Japanese intellectuals. The Legends of Tōno strikes a universal
humanistic chord in the Japanese psyche. This is evident in its continued popularity. Revolutionary politics, culture and psychology
mix in strange ways in the Japanese modern mind. Folklore and Yanagita's career touches each one of these elements in distinctive ways.

Yanagita and the Meiji Literary World

Yanagita's older brother Michiyasu (a student of Matsunami
Yuzan and a member of the politician Yamagita Aritomo's poetry group,

the <u>Tokiwakai</u>) first introduced him into the literary life of Tokyo. It was Michiyasu who selected Kunio's poetry teacher and then introduced him to Mori Ōgai, Kōda Rohan and other leading writers of the day. Michiyasu and Kunio saw poetry in a special way: they maintained that poetry should be understood with the feelings of the times. The subject matter of poetry, they felt, should be found in experience, not in books. Since most poetry of the day was artificial and its range of vocabulary was limited, they tried to give expression to new feelings by composing poems in the vocabulary of the era. Feelings were to be pure and fresh, vocabulary accurate and appropriate. Michiyasu distinguished between the methods of poetry and the requirements of scholarship. The vital elements for <u>poetry</u> were the conception of an idea, sensitivity to shades of meaning, and insight. <u>Scholarship</u> required knowledge, insight and common sense. The common element in scholarship and poetry as Michiyasu and Kunio both saw it was "insight"--the intuitive or psychological grasp of essentials. Folklore studies, as those who are familiar with the field will recognize, is a discipline that relies heavily on insight and uses literary as well as other resources. In his own work Yanagita employed many literary devices.[4]

If one had to pick a year both critical for Yanagita's later career and meaningful in terms of a dramatic change in his outlook on life, it would be 1896, the year he entered Tokyo Imperial University and the year both his parents passed away. The loss of his parents, especially of his mother, who was his model for a cultural transmitter, threw Yanagita into a deep state of melancholy. As he expressed it, "I lost all desire for doing anything." He expressed his grief by turning to what he knew best; he immersed himself in literature. He also took to making long trips to the remote regions of Japan. As Kijima Yasuo, the outstanding Japanese interpreter of Yanagita's

---

4. Yanagita's brand of folklore emphasized the modern expressive, oral tradition. Other scholars focused on <u>material</u> folk culture and the use of folklore evidence for philological studies of <u>classical</u> literature.

poetic career, points out, from this time on Yanagita's poetic vocabulary underwent a transformation; he became more concerned with death and the darker side of human experience.[5] The theme of death is prominent in the Legends of Tōno and reappears vividly in Yanagita's later works, especially About Our Ancestors.

Yanagita, an enthusiastic twenty-one-year-old college student, plunged into literature at the peak of the Meiji-era fascination with Western literature. Tayama Katai, the leader of the naturalist literary movement and close friend of Yanagita, captured the excitement of the times in his memoirs, Thirty Years in Tokyo, 1917:

> It was fascinating how the different streams of European literature entered Japan. Into the midst of the small peaceful world of 3,000 years of insularity, Bushido and Confucianism, Buddhism and superstition, giri (duty) and ninjō (human feeling), humiliating sacrifice and endurance, compromise and social intercourse, came Nietzche's unsparing criticism, Ibsen's resistance, Tolstoy's ego, and Zola's dissection.

Yanagita and his friends (Kunikida Doppo, Shimazaki Tōson, Tayama and others) spent their time scouring Maruzen Bookstore, known for its stock of foreign books, for the latest foreign-language editions of Western literature. Every new book led to a period of intense reading, long evening debates and eventually a book review in a popular journal of the day.

Yanagita's poetry, from very early on, reflected a restrained manner of expression. For him, poetry was a vehicle in the creation of verbal impression; poetry was not, however, to be a vehicle for expressing very personal inner feelings. Kunio's images were traditional; the emphasis was on a world, often quite dreary, behind external appearances.

It was about the turn of the century that Yanagita began to experiment with different literary forms. At one point he became

---

5. Kijima Yasuo, Mori no Fukuro (1982) explores Yanagita's literary career in a systematic and thoughtful manner.

interested in Russian literature. He also founded the Ibsen Society in Japan.

It is important to understand one literary trend, "naturalist literature," to appreciate why Yanagita wrote The Legends of Tōno and why he eventually abandoned literature as the mode for exploring and expressing his interest in Japanese culture. Tayama Katai (1872-1930) is credited with introducing the word "naturalism" into the Japanese literary vocabulary; it had several interpretations in Japan, but for Tayama it meant an individualism that was opposed to the repressive conventions of society.

The naturalists, all of whom had participated in the mid-Meiji romantic poetry movement, attempted to combine the realistic (natural) portrayal of an individual in his environment with a single character (protagonist) point of view. The main characters in naturalist writing suffer at the hands of society--they are frustrated by family pressures, the individual is alone and isolated in rural society, or, for women, they are doomed to living in the world of men. The descriptive technique employed was called byōsha, and emphasized passivity and impressionism.

The Search for a Literature of Social Protest

Yanagita, as a Meiji intellectual who believed in the importance of education, wanted to have an impact on the course of modern Japan. Like so many talented Japanese in the modern era, he tried to shape history by subtle psychological and literary means, not through political action. Naturally, writing was important to him. Yanagita wanted to write a novel and turned to writing The Legends of Tōno, thinking of it as a point of departure for a distinctively different literary form--a literary form that would have a qualitatively different impact on its readers. It is important to understand that Yanagita assumed an integral relationship between the "high culture," namely the national literary tradition, and the body of folk culture produced by the peasantry. This is evident in his literary rendering of folk legends in The Legends of Tōno. He had a Japanese version of Grimm's Fairy Tales in mind when he wrote it. By challenging the prevailing Meiji literary trends, Yanagita tried to ensure the vitality of Japan's literary tradition by bringing rural, agricultural traditions to national (urban) literary attention.

Yanagita knew better than anyone else that he was waging a solitary and probably losing battle. The first indication we get that Yanagita recognized the difficulty of his task is in a passage from Kropotkin he included in his 1909 essay "Kropotkin and Turgenev":

> In a brilliant lecture on Hamlet and Don Quixote, Turgenev divided the history makers of mankind into two classes, represented by one or the other of the following characteristics. "Analysis first of all, and then egotism, and therefore no faith--an egotist cannot even believe in himself": so he characterized Hamlet. "Therefore he is a skeptic,and never will achieve anything; while Don Quixote, who fights against windmills and takes a barber's plate for the magic helmet of Mambrino (who of us has never made the same mistake?), is a leader of the masses, because the masses always follow those who, taking no heed of the sarcasms of the majority, or even of persecutions, march straight forward, keeping their eyes fixed upon a goal which is seen, perhaps, by no one but themselves. They search, they fall, but they rise again, and find it.

Anyone familiar with Yanagita's career would recognize the "Don Quixote" dimension to his character. A decade later, in 1919, in his book Rites, Festivals and Society (Sairei to seken), Yanagita again singled out the example of Western literature to make a point, this time it was from Ibsen's An Enemy of the People. In the play, a lone doctor, impetuous, irrational, and driven by his heart, stands against the false morality of the bourgeoisie. Yanagita understood Ibsen's message and was moved by the closing line of the play in which the doctor says, "The strongest man in the world is he who stands most alone." Yanagita was a talented and stubborn individual who pursued his mission with singular devotion. He worked by himself and had no outstanding disciples; his long trips into the rural regions of Japan, the many photographs of him off in the corner of his library smoking while he wrote, and the incessant complaints about his studying from his wife all testify to this quality.

By 1909, when Yanagita was putting the finishing touches on The Legends of Tōno, the literary world had reached a richness and diversity formerly unknown.[6] Nagai Kafū had published his Tales of America (Amerika monogatari) and Tales of France (Furansu monogatari), works highly critical of what he saw as the false civilization of Meiji Japan. The new literary journals of Mitabungaku and Shira kaba were founded about the same time that Natsume Sōseki published his book And Then (Sorekara). Ōgai's Vita Sexualis and Ueda Bin's Vortex (Uzumaki) had also just appeared. The naturalist movement was out of fashion and the urban, elite-based novel was the main concern. Russian literature was now more in vogue,

Yanagita thought that effective literature could serve a social function. In the essay "Kropotkin and Turgenev" Yanagita spoke in praise of the consciousness-raising role of Russian literature:

> Russian literature, especially the modern literature, always reflects social conditions, and Russian authors, to varying degrees, have revolutionary tendencies. Art is given a fresh vitality in collision with the social system. The Russians have great imaginations and an audacity to go ahead and try to actualize their ideals.

Japanese literature seemed to lack something. In his essay "The Fiction Civil Servants Read," Yanagita pointed out that, for some reason, as distinct from China and Russia, in Japan the realms of politics and literature remained apart. Interestingly, the situation seems the same in Japan today. Somehow young urban writers did not write about things that appealed to the older generation which had grown up in the rural areas. He advised that young writers

---

6. The background to Yanagita's writing of The Legends of Tōno and some interpretation of its unique qualities can be found in my essay in Tembō, March 1976 and in the introduction to my translation of the book (Japan Foundation Translation Series, 1975).

be sent to the provinces to describe rural life so that they could write literature relevant to Japanese society as a whole. It must be remembered that at this time Japan was an agrarian society, and nearly everyone spent his or her formative years in a village setting.

It was while searching for a new mode of expression, one that could convey both psychology and drama, that another aspiring young writer, Sasaki Kizen (1896-1933), visited Yanagita and told him tales and legends from the Tono district of Iwate Prefecture. Yanagita took down the legends from Sasaki and then decided to go to Tono in August 1909 to verify for himself what the area of Tono was like. Yanagita's short "essay" at the beginning of The Legends of Tono was a new technique for a Japanese writer. This "essay form," borrowed from Western literature, had the flexibility Yanagita needed to express the character of village life. In a 1907 essay, "The Literary Sketch and the Essay," Yanagita had written that the essay style of sketching reality, free of decoration or invention, represented a whole new literary genre for Japan. In writing an essay one first felt, looked, listened, thought, and only then was one ready to write. This is the method Yanagita employed in reworking the local legends into a literary form that he felt would be read by informed Japanese and move them to give serious consideration and respect to Japan's indigenous folk tradition.

When Yanagita wrote The Legends of Tono he considered it literature--literature that captured nature and rural life in its subjective aspects. He hoped to drive the reader into action. History indicated he failed. This was Yanagita's first, and unfortunately last, effort at sustained literature. The work never satisfied his literary friends. Tayama, one of his staunchest critics, wrote about the Tono book in his column, "The Inkpot":

> Yanagita's work has an impressionistic quality.
> While Kunio maintains that I, a naturalist writer,
> cannot understand his feelings and am not really
> qualified to evaluate his work, I find the work

infused with an extravagance of affected rusticity.
I remain unmoved. His use of on-site observation to
create the background in an essay is significant.
The work's impressionistic and artistic qualities,
however, derive more from the treatment of the data
than the actual content.

What Yanagita did do, however, was to write a moving piece of
literature that touched a sensitive, nationalistic nerve in the
Japanese psyche. The readers unfortunately turned inward. The work
has a haiku-like quality about it, and the narrative movement is
determined by the juxtaposition and reversal of short scenes or
thought sequences, much like classical Japanese literature. The
reader does experience a certain excitement as he gropes for a perspective that will lend meaning to the collection of legends. The
language of the original is a dignified colloquial, emphasizing
visual rather than verbal imagery. Still, if this was intended as a
political as well as literary document, it did not have the desired
result. The 350 copies of the work Yanagita printed at his own ex-
pense were distributed to friends. It wasn't until the 1930s that
the book was actually published commercially.

The Legends of Tōno as Literature

A variety of arguments can be made for the continued literary
appeal of the Legends in Japan--explanations about what appeals to
Japanese emotions and sensibilities. Let me just mention some dimensions of the work which, I feel, help us understand Yanagita's
method. First, there is the nearly physical quality of what I would
call the creation of an atmosphere or environment. Some people refer
to this quality of Yanagita's style as a "psychic landscape" (shinshō
fūkei). There is an emphasis on experience enhanced by the lack of
clear-cut subject-object distinctions in the Japanese language. The
Japanese is also more abstract.

Kishimoto Hideo, the late Professor of Religion at Tokyo University, explained this quality in the following way:

Suppose a man is taking a walk in the countryside of
Japan. He is surrounded in quiet autumn scenery.
Some sentiment comes to his mind. He feels it and
wants to express the sentiment. He would say
"sabishii" (lonesome).

What he says on such an occasion can be simply this
one word. This single word can well be regarded as
a complete statement in the Japanese language. For
the Japanese language, a full sentence in the Western grammatical sense is not ordinarily called for.
. . . It is not necessary in Japanese to specify the
subject by explicitly stating whether "I" am feeling
lonesome, or "the scenery" is lonesome. Without
such analysis, one's sentiment can be projected
there in its immediate form. . . . One of the characteristics of the Japanese language is to be able
to project man's experience in its immediate and
unanalyzed form.[7]

Yanagita, a very introverted person, preferred an impersonal atmosphere to the expression of deep personal emotion. In his work,
culture is absorbed into nature--a nature that represents the unconscious collective experience of the Japanese people.

Some mention should be made here about what Japanese writers
define as the unique, emotional tendencies of the Japanese intellect.
They point to the Japanese preference for handling issues within a
psychological and social nexus rather than resort to abstract thinking. The philosopher Nakamura Hajime has summarized what he considers the irrational tendencies of the Japanese mentality: a disre-
gard for logical rules, a fondness for symbolic expression, a dis-
regard of the objective order, and a general preference for an
intuitive or emotional way of thinking.

A second quality that I find of interest in The Legends of Tono
centers on the distinction between the social behavior and belief of
the villagers and high religion (shūkyō). In this dualism the ethical code is not, as in Western religion, an index of the vitality of
the religion. Yanagita distinguished between "belief" (shinkō) and

---

7. "Some Japanese Cultural Traits and Religions," in The
Japanese Mind, edited by Charles A. Moore (1967).

"religion" (shūkyō). He preferred shinko which meant to him a living tradition transmitted by direct feeling. In his view Buddhism and Christianity were religions (shūkyō) which were similar in character to the "man-made" moral system of Meiji Confucianism, which he objected to. As any reader of it will soon recognize, filial piety, loyalty, industriousness and thrift had no place in the moral system of The Legends of Tōno. Man's struggle with nature requires a different set of norms. What sets these legends off from other diary and tale literature is also the fact that the peasantry, despite its character, is not the object of scorn and ridicule. The strength and simplicity of the peasantry is emphasized. Instead of moralizing about what "should" be, we find in the legends ideas of discord, unfilial behavior, fraud, self-interest, protest, arrogance and distrust. A man kills his mother; someone shoots a god; a man eats his children; children desert their old father; the greedy manipulate religion; relatives steal from other family members; priests are killed; sisters kill each other; kappa (ugly water creatures) impregnate women and the offspring are hacked to pieces; witchcraft is a source of village authority. This cluster of negative, primary emotions is presented as a part of man's struggle both with himself and with nature. Yanagita, at least in this work, saw morality as dependent upon the primary tension between man and nature. If Yanagita were alive today, he would probably take on those who point only to the positive effects of Japan's trying to be "number one" in the world. He would also discuss a different layer of the Japanese psyche--a dimension of the national psychology people tend to ignore.

Another aspect of the work can be found in the coming and going of religious forces. This is of great importance when one considers Yanagita's overall approach. In later folklore writings, he used the term "emotional or psychological phenomena" (shinri genshō) to explain what he meant by the religious experience. Yanagita's early training brought him into contact with the learning of the National Learning (kokugaku) school of the scholar Hirata Atsutane (1776-1843). Hirata was one of the first scholars to give serious con-

sideration to the world of kami, tengu (goblins) and ghosts. Hirata
distinguished between the dark nether-world (yomi-no-kuni) and the
more fluid relationship existing between the world of spirits and the
domain of man. Yanagita, like Hirata, was present minded and viewed
the "here and now" world as a place where kami tested people. Movement between the "here and now" and the "next world" was referred to
as moving between the visible and the concealed (kenyu).

In 1905 Yanagita wrote a very important essay, "On the Concept
of the Concealed and the Mysterious in Shinto Thought" (Yūmeidan).
In this essay he discussed the hidden or mysterious world of the kami
as the most important and perhaps most neglected aspect of Japanese
folk religion. In the essay on the concealed and mysterious, Yanagita mentioned Heinrich Heine's book, Gods in Exile. Yanagita was
impressed by the comparisons with Japan; the book showed that the
Greek gods Jupiter, Mars, and Venus had been defeated by higher
religion (Christianity) and had retreated into the uninhabited
mountains. Heine, in fact, opened his Gods in Exile with the statement, "I am speaking here of that metamorphosis into demons which the
Greek and Roman gods underwent when Christianity achieved supreme
control of the world." One is immediately reminded of Yanagita's
thesis that primitive survivals of ancient Japanese religion could
still be found in the remote, mountainous regions of Japan.

Conclusion

The Legends of Tōno, and to a lesser extent Yanagita's other
writings, is powerful literature to Japanese. This graphic presentation of the Japanese spirit in literary form, packed with traditional
religious symbolism and spiced with theoretical hints at historical
explanation, is at the core of Yanagita's folklore writings and explains the appeal of his works to some critical, and many more un-
critical but struggling, modern intellects in Japan. Yanagita himself
opted for evolution, not revolution, and scholars and thinkers
attracted to him have thought in similar ways. He clearly addresses

basic human concerns in a way that has intellectual appeal, at least in Japan.

Yanagita, as his wise and loyal folklore disciples point out, and I would tend to agree, has been used by alienated Japanese intellectuals in their search for an indigenous critical or revolutionary tradition. More than being the original thinker or systematizer of folklore studies that he is often characterized as, Yanagita stands as a sensitive literary mind that satisfied the illogical, aesthetic yearnings of modern men in search of a tradition against which to measure the course of modern Japan. The restoration of the wholism of the village, the joy of local festivals and the commonality of shared experience is the hope that Yanagita holds out to urban, tired and bored Japanese.

All of this is important, I believe, to understand Yanagita's true place in modern Japanese intellectual history. These interpretations and his popularity must be distinguished from the real Yanagita. One must separate Yanagita the folk hero from the Yanagita of particular historical contexts if one is to understand his actual folklore contribution and methodology. One must go to the original Yanagita to critique his scholarship. Secondary sources will not help. Only by careful study can we sort out the myth from the reality and return to the question, "Are there lessons for comparative analysis in the Japanese folklore tradition as represented by Yanagita Kunio?" Yanagita does not, in my view, stand up well under the scrutiny of Western social science examination. But the secret of his genius and his intention in founding folklore studies had very little to do with founding an academic discipline. Yanagita's mission was to revitalize the Japanese sensibility from the bottom up. He was been successful in moving people to appreciate Japanese tradition and somewhat less successful in generating the kind of social change he envisioned. This and this alone accounts for his celebration in Japan. It may also explain his limited appeal abroad.

YANAGITA AND HIS WORKS

Yoneyama Toshinao

I. Introduction

Let me begin by recalling some remarks made by the television director for a program about Yanagita Kunio. It was in June 1974, one year before Yanagita's name suddenly became widely known as a result of several events marking the centenary of his birth. The program was planned by Mr. Soeda Masataka of the Japanese public broadcasting corporation, or NHK, which is a nationwide network with a special channel for educational programs. Mr. Soeda and two other directors of the educational section of the Osaka Station came to me during the planning stage, and I suggested they ask the help of Professor Itoh Kanji, of the National Museum of Ethnology.

Once Prof. Itoh agreed to join our project, we created a series that was shown as part of the "Citizen's University" at 8:00 p.m. every Thursday. We invited many people to talk on the program; some joined us in the studio, others we interviewed on film. They included Kuwabara Takeo, Aruga Kizaemon, Wakamori Tarō, Miyamoto Tsuneichi, Kamishima Jirō, and many others, some of whom have since passed away. Mr. Soeda and his colleagues travelled around the country to collect materials related to Yanagita and his accomplishments, and I was able to participate in their fieldwork for the program we filmed at Tsujikawa, in Hyōgo-ken, where Yanagita was born. It was my first visit to that community, and I learned a great deal from the trip. Indeed, it was my participation in that program that marked me as a person interested in Yanagita Kunio, resulting in my invitation to this workshop. So I must express my gratitude to the program and its director.

I will not say much about the program here, but simply recall the director's words. He said that the reason he began to make a program about Yanagita Kunio was that he saw Yanagita's books at practically every house he visited. You see, because of his occupation he had occasion to visit the homes of professors, literary critics, writers, journalists, artists, and other kinds of professional intellectuals. And everywhere, he found Yanagita's works on his host's bookshelf, whether the person was politically progressive or conservative, young or old, social scientist or not. The director was keenly interested in this phenomenon and began to wonder why it was so.

Doubtless, it is a kind of snobbery on our part to have such books. Similarly, when I was a graduate student, many of my friends had the collected works of Marx and Engels. Indeed, it was standard practice to own them, even though poor students like me could not afford to. It is no wonder, then, that one can now see Yanagita's works on everyone's bookshelf. His collected works were published in 36 volumes by Chikuma Shobō between 1968 and 1971, and many people, including myself, have purchased them. They do, in fact, take up a conspicuous amount of room on one's book shelf.

However, I think what Mr. Soeda noticed amounts to more than just a fad among Japanese intellectuals. Yanagita Kunio has been very popular among a wide range of people, including communists, anarchists, ultra-nationalists, and all political shades in between. Of course, there are those in Japan who do not appreciate the writings of Yanagita. Some flatly criticize him as a haughty authoritarian. But it seems that in general, intellectuals enjoy reading his works. I, myself, feel that I do not trust a person who has no sense of appreciation for Yanagita's writings. I also sometimes wonder if it is really possible to translate the emic content of his works into other languages, and other cultural contexts. The "translation of culture" is supposed to be the speciality of anthropologists like myself, but such a person as Yanagita drives us into a corner.

Let me introduce several aspects of the man and his works against the background of his life history. The following section headings provide a tentative method of periodizing the 88 years of his life. A chronological table showing his life span in relation to contemporary events would demonstrate that he lived through almost the entire modern history of Japan.

II. The Life History

1. Fukuzaki: A Crossroad in Banshū

Yanagita Kunio left an autobiographical work among his last publications. The title of the book, "Kokyō Nanajūnen," or "My Hometown, Seventy Years," is somewhat ambiguous as it is not clear if it means "the town seventy years later," or "my life for 70 years after I left the town," or "70 years of my hometown." It is not a conventional autobiography because it originated in a series of Yanagita's interviews with an old friend, recorded and edited by one of his disciples. Nevertheless, it does reveal his life history as he related it.

Yanagita was born on July 31, 1875 (Meiji 8), at Tsujikawa, Fukuzakichō. At that time, the community was called Tsujikawa, Shintō-gun, Tawaramura. He was the sixth and last son of Matsuoka Kenji and his wife Take. The fourth and fifth sons had died at the ages of two and four, respectively, but Kunio had two elder brothers ten years or more older than he, and two younger brothers who were both closer to him in age: Shizuo, three years younger, and Teruo, six years younger. Apparently, all of them were distinguished individuals. The eldest brother, who left home to settle in Fukawa, Ibaraki-ken as a medical doctor, took care of all the younger brothers. The second eldest, Inoue Michiyasu, finally became chief of the Outadokoro, in charge of poems in the imperial court. Although it sounds like a strange job to hold in the court bureaucracy, it is in fact a rather important post considering that the Emperor and Empress Meiji were both very fond of composing uta, or Japanese short poems. Through him, young Kunio was able to meet and befriend many writers and poets. Matsuoka Shizuo, the younger brother closest to him in age, became an officer in the navy, and wrote ethnographies on the Pacific Islands. His youngest brother, Matsuoka Eikyū, became a famous Japanese-style painter.

The community of Tsujikawa is located at the junction of two major roads: one a traditional highway from the Kyoto-Osaka area to Kyūshū, extending as far as Nagasaki and Kagoshima, the other a road connecting the Inland Sea area to the northern Japanese sea coast. More precisely, the town is located at the intersection of routes from Tottori to Kyoto and from Himeji to Ikuno, where there used to be a silver mine.

His father was a poor, local intellectual, who practiced medicine and also assumed the role of Shinto priest. His house was located at the edge of town and Yanagita describes it as the "smallest house in Japan." He says:

> My eldest brother, Kanae, married a girl at the age of twenty. She came from a neighboring vil lage. However, our house had no space for two couples at once. My mother was strong and rigid, and it is natural that two couples would find it difficult to survive together. In that era, a mother-in-law would always defeat her daughter-in-law in family conflicts, so within a year my brother's wife escaped back to her parental home, and my brother began to drink. Since the Matsuoka house had produced a series of medical specialists, my parents sold some land and a house to send him to a school of medicine--a quick course attached to Tokyo Imperial University. There he could learn medicine without having to use German. At the age of 26, he graduated from the school, but as he would need money to open a medical practice there, and since several medical doctors related to him were there already, he had no intention of returning to his home town. So, instead, he married a woman from an old family in Ibaraki-ken and

succeeded to the house of a doctor in a town called
Fukawa.

He has since returned only once to Tsujikawa,
his birth place, and that thirty years later. By
that time, he had lost the local dialect and accent.
When I recall the tragic fate of my brother, I want
to tell others that the house where I was born was
the smallest house in Japan. It is possible to say
that my intention to study Japanese Folklore has
emerged from that fate and the smallness of that
house.[1]

Yanagita also recalls, among other things, that he once stayed
on the second floor of an old house in the community. It was owned
by the head of the Miki family, which had provided the village mayor
for more than 300 years. While he lived at this house, he devoted
himself to reading the collection of books stored on its second
floor. He was often so silent that some members of the household
wondered if he was not asleep. He says his taste for browsing
through books must have begun from this experience.

I visited Tsujikawa for the first time in 1974, and now I bring
my students there once a year. The community has a typical settle-
ment pattern for the Banshū region, and consists of a warm, sunny,
tranquil, small basin surrounded by mild hills covered by pine trees.
After visiting there, I feel I can sympathize with his statement during an interview that after his death he wanted to linger on the
sunny side of the hill behind his native community, to watch what
people were doing below in the basin.

2. Fukawa: His Discovery of Poverty

He stayed with his parents until the age of thirteen, and then
in 1887 moved to Fukawa, where his eldest brother was practicing
medicine. Another brother accompanied him. At that time there was
no Tokaidō-line train, so they took a boat from Kobe to Yokohama.

---

1. Teihon Yanagita Kunio shū, bekkan 3, p. 17.

Yanagita stayed for three years at Fukawa, a small port on the River Tone (Ibaraki-ken, Kitasoma-gun, Tonegawa, Fukawa, is its full address). There, he found many features of life that differed from those of his birthplace in Banshū, the mild inland sea area. First, he found that children called each other by their first names only, while in Tsujikawa everyone had attached honorary terms of address, except for very close relatives. He was called "Kunio" in Fukawa, where before he had been called "Kunyo-han," or at least "Kuni-yan." Furthermore, he found that in Fukawa every house had only two children and people were surprised when he told them he had eight brothers. They said, "How can you survive with such a large number of children?" So he understood the reason they adopted the two-child system, even while he was still a child himself. He writes:

> The area suffered serious damage from famine forty or fifty years ago. When people faced shortages of food, the only arrangement they could make was "death." Japan maintained a population ceiling of 30,000,000 until 1880, and that was accomplished by means of a vulgar method of birth control, less decent than methods used today. The famine of Tenmei devastated the area along the River Tone, and although there were not many documents left to tell of the next famine, the famine of Tenpō, it seems that people had suffered from the later one even before they fully recovered from the first.

> I was often told that people of Fukawa had come to his eldest brother to ask for a death certificate. He had, however, refused in most cases.

> My clearest memory of life along the River Tone is of a small temple to Jizō, a Buddhist patron deity of children. There, at the righthand side of the deity, I found a votive plaque. It pictured a woman who had just sent off her baby, killing it with her hands pressed on its body. Her shadow, falling on a screen behind her, had horns on its head. A Jizō standing nearby was crying. I remember that I understood the meaning of the painting and felt a chill.[2]

2. Ibid., p. 21.

He also says that he experienced the difficulty of hunger, which led him to study folklore, and also motivated him to become a bureaucrat in the Ministry of Agriculture and Commerce.

There are clearcut differences in productivity between the southwestern and northeastern parts of Japan. The former can produce two or more crops in a year, whereas the latter yields only once. And up to the 1920s even that one crop (rice) was very unstable because of the weather. This ecological condition is an important factor making for variety in ways of life, particularly at a time when people relied largely on agricultural production per se. I think Yanagita found a culture of poverty in the Kantō Plain when he came to Fukawa, and through contrasting it to the Banshū, he may have begun to be interested in the differences within Japanese culture.

3. His Debut in the Literary World

His elder brother, Inoue Michiyasu, entered the Medical Department of Tokyo Imperial University and specialized in ophthalmology. But at the same time, he had many friends among poets and writers. (He finally ended up as a scholar of the classics Manyōshū and Harima-Fūdoki, while in charge of poetry at the Imperial Court.) In 1892, Yanagita moved to Tokyo to follow his elder brother, and after attending several schools finally entered First Higher School in 1897.

Through the elder brother, he came to know such writers as Kunikida Doppo (1871-1908) Tayama Katai (1871-1930), and Shimazaki Tōson (1872-1943). He wrote poems and even published an anthology with five friends. He also composed some waka, short-form poems, and some others that were published in several magazines of the literary world.

Although his specialty at the university was agricultural policy, which he studied in the department of political science in the Faculty of Law, he maintained his friendships and involvement in the literary world. Some say that Yanagita Kunio was one of the leading members of the literary world in the last years of Meiji from 1900 to 1910.

However, after he became established as the founder of Japanese Folklore Studies, he tended to conceal, or at least avoid showing, his poetic works. He did not include them in his collected works at all. His poems are romantic lyrics. I do not see any reason to avoid showing them, but this was his attitude toward his own works of poetry. Prof. Ishida Eiichirō once said that the scientist Yanagita could not overcome the poet Yanagita, and that is why his scholarly works never achieved their goal.[3] It seems to me that the poet Yanagita is his most substantial part, and that his works on Japanese culture are inseparable from this poetic nature.

In fact, after leaving public service he would begin a new life centered on writing with a new assignment from Asahi Shinbun, one of Japan's leading newspapers. I think his literary career must have played an important role in getting him this new appointment.

4. An Adopted Son to the Yanagita Family

Matsuoka Kunio had been adopted by the Yanagita family in 1901 (Meiji 34), when he was 27. That is the same year he was appointed as an official of the Ministry of Agriculture and Commerce, one of the main divisions of the imperial government, which later was split into several ministries.

The Yanagita family was an old lineage from Shinshū, or Nagano perfecture, but as Yanagita Naohei lived in Tokyo, it had nothing to do with its hometown except probably to take care of graves and property. It was common in that period for a certain class of people to maintain their lineages, and for that purpose to adopt a promising young man as a yōshi, or an adopted son, by providing a girl of the family as his spouse. This could be considered just a matter of "marrying in," but as Yanagita's case clearly indicates, the adoption

3. E. Ishida, "Unfinished but Enduring--Yanagita Kunio's Folklore Studies," Japan Quarterly, Vol. X, No. 1, 1963.

took place first, and then there was a marriage to a daughter. Yanagita, for example, married Ko, Yanagita Naohei's fourth daughter, three years after he was adopted in 1904.

Out of the eight sons in the Matsuoka family, two died in infancy, one died at the age of 19, and two, Kunio and Inoue Michiyasu, became yōshi to other families, and changed their surnames. Only the two younger brothers of Yanagita Kunio went on to form their own branches of the Matsuoka family.

I do not know much about the personal affairs of the Yanagita family. Some say that Ko was not a good wife and that is why he travelled a lot. Yamaguchi Masao once wrote that Mrs. Yanagita was counted as one of three bad wives in the area where Yanagita lived, but I imagine that they maintained the standard upper-middle-class family life of modern Tokyo people during the early 20th century. In About Our Ancestors, there are several passages describing the Yanagita family and its ancestors. That is, about half a century later he described it as if it were his own family, but with no particular sentiment attached.

5. A Bureaucrat of the Meiji Government

In 1901, the same year he became a Yanagita, he was appointed as an official of the Ministry of Agriculture and Commerce. It is hard to judge if he was an able bureaucrat or not. What he did seems to me to have been mostly clerical work, or mere administrative things, rather than policy making. He held his post in the government for eighteen years and resigned in 1919 at the age of 45. Some say that he quarreled with the chairman of the upper house while he was the secretary general, and finally resigned his post. In 1910 (Meiji 43), he joined a group called the Kyōdokai, which was attended by some leading policy makers of the central government, such as Ishiguro Tadaatsu, Odauchi Michitoshi, Kimura Shūzō, Ono Takeo, Nitobe Inazō, and Makiguchi Tsunesaburō (the founder of Sōka Gakkai in later years). And, as we shall see, he wrote prolifically on rural affairs while he was in the government. Hence, he might have had some influence on such policies as those having to do with agricultural cooperatives. But he seems to have played a minor role on the bureaucratic social ladder. He concentrated on reading documents in the Cabinet Library, accessible only to elite bureaucrats in the central government. Another merit to being a government official was that he would be provided with many conveniences anywhere he went in the country. He started to deliver speeches in many parts of the country and could meet people of all localities. It was a great privilege for him to see the different parts of Japan.

6. Early Publications

The activities of the Kyōdokai coincide with Yanagita's early publications. Although he published several books, including such titles as Nōseigaku (Agricultural Policy, 1902), Nōgyō seisakugaku (The Study of Agricultural Policy, 1902), and Nihon sandō shiryaku (A Short History of Copper Mining in Japan, 1903), his first important publication was Nochino Karikotoba no ki (Hunting Terminology, 1909). It is a glossary of terms used by hunters in Shiiba-mura, Miyazaki-ken. He published it by himself. Then, in 1910, he published "Tōno-monogatari," the Legends of Tōno, using materials provided by Sasaki Kizen. He visited the Tōno basin in 1909, and this made it possible to write a nice set of introductory remarks for the collection of tales. It first contained 119 legends, and then 229 more were added as addenda. Kuwabara Takeo remarks that the Legends of Tōno is one of the important literary products of the age. Some of Yanagita's literary friends described themselves as "naturalists," but Yanagita left that school and attempted to write in his own way. The style is plain, elegant, narrative, with echoes from the Edo Period.

These early publications had great appeal and collecting them was important and meaningful. But they are not for the general reader. It is important to note that the Legends of Tōno, published privately in a few hundred copies, was dedicated by the author "to my friends abroad." This may have several meanings, but to us these are impressive words. By the end of the Meiji Period modern Japan had become almost another country, so different was it from the beginning of Meiji. Thus, the term "abroad" can be interpreted in this sense. It seems to me that the remarkable achievement of the book is in its quality as a record of oral traditions that were almost forgotten with the passing of time. Yanagita was the first to excavate the rock of Japanese oral tradition that is deposited in the subliminal world of Japanese, and it seems to me that his own great contribution was this conscious effort to "write down" an oral tradition. By means of this effort, one can appreciate fantastic stories from marginal parts of Japan as if they were from one's own hometown.

Most likely, Yanagita availed himself of the last chance history offered to collect such tales. There were still active at that time some old people, born before the Meiji Restoration, who remembered what they had heard from parents or grandparents. Most of those who had absorbed modern knowledge and sciences imported from abroad would hardly notice the importance of those folk traditions, not only because they thought they were useless, superstitious, and primitive, but also because they had heard such tales, in ample numbers, from someone nearby. Yet Yanagita knew, I think, that they would disappear if they were abandoned as before. Moreover, I think he went on to an even more interesting endeavor, which is the comparison of such tales. In the beginning, he had the simple intention to present hidden aspects of the Japanese mind that could be described using the tales as a resource. He succeeded in writing a nice book, which certainly appealed to some Japanese who had already lost their hometowns and oral traditions.

7. His Concern for Rural Affairs

As mentioned above, he had his own clear motivations for taking a job with the central government. I do not know if he was able to achieve his goals in the government, but at least it is clear that he publicly demonstrated concern for rural affairs.

The same year he published Legends of Tōno, he also published a collection of essays on agricultural policy, entitled Jidai to Nōsei (The Present Age and Agricultural Policy, 1910). It is a professional book on contemporary policies regarding tenants, landlords, management, the family farm system, finance, cooperative associations, and so forth. It is very clear that in the beginning his intentions were closer to real policy application and enforcement in order to help the rural population to do something with their lives. But just after he became a bureaucrat, he began gradually to shift from the hasty application of policy to a tendency to investigate the situation carefully, more objectively, and in a wider context. A decade later he wrote on similar subjects but his attitude, or approach to the subject, is very different from the earlier collection of essays. Toshi to nōson (The City and Agrarian Villages, 1929), Meiji-Taishō shi: sesō-hen (A History of the Meiji and Taishō Periods: Social Affairs, 1931), and Nihon nōmin-shi (A History of Japanese Agriculturalists, 1931) are all unique products, in a distinctively "Yanagita" style. They show his deep concern for ordinary people, whom he called jōmin, and their welfare. But compared to those books published ten years or more earlier, the style is more detached, and emphasis is more upon tradition rather than new ideas.

Let me add a few words on Yanagita's notion of the jōmin, or common people. Yanagita used the word as early as 1900, but it was first used almost synonymously with the terms heimin or shomin. Jō (constant) is the opposite of "variable," and min is the opposite of kan, meaning officials, or the public sector. But after 1932, the word jōmin was used more often in Yanagita's writings than the other words, and it denoted almost every Japanese, including all classes and occupations. From 1930 to 1935, the word became fixed in Yanagita's folklore studies. Some assume that its development had some relation to the political situation of the period, wherein even "work societies" or "social work" were confused with leftist notions and indiscriminately suppressed by the ruling power.

8. Yanagita Kunio as a Tourist

Yanagita placed heavy emphasis on observation as a necessary complement to reading books and documents. He traveled the country very extensively and suggested to his disciples that they do likewise. He also wrote several important works on journeys: Kainan shoki (A note on the south-seas) in 1925, Yukiguni no haru (Spring in Snow Country) in 1928, and Shūfū-chō (A note on autumn wind) in 1932.

He followed three stages in his studies: 1) observation with the eyes, 2) interview by means of language, 3) thinking with the mind. 1) is for the tourist, 2) is for visiting residents, and 3) is for people who live in the locale. His emphasis on "field work" is unique in the Japanese academic world, which is predominantly oriented to laboratory work or library studies. In this sense, he was one pioneer of Japanese anthropological sciences.

9. Commitment to "Japanese Folklore"

Yanagita's interest in the oral tradition began to develop in 1909, and accelerated through his participation in the Kyōdokai (in 1910), and editing of the journal Kyōdo kenkyū (1913-17). But his real commitment began in the 1920s. He resigned from the government in 1919 at the age of 45 and became a visiting member of the Asahi Shinbun next year. He asked the newspaper company to let him travel freely for a couple of years. He then went on several important journeys, which included Europe in 1921 and 1922. In 1922, he organized a group called Nantō Kenkyūkai (Research Group on the Southern Islands) and in 1924 another group called Hoppō Bunmei Kenkyūkai (Research Group on Northern Civilization). Then, in 1925, at the age of 51, he started the journal Minzoku, which was published until 1928. Dr. Aruga Kizaemon remarks that this was the beginning of all anthropological studies in Japan, stimulating the work of Origuchi

Shinobu, Kintaichi Kyōsuke, Nakayama Tarō, Iha Fuyu, Ishida Mikino-suke, Tanabe Juri, Okudaira Takehiko, Oka Masao and Aruga himself. They also started a serial publication called Rohen Sōsho.

Itoh Kanji divides the scholarly works of Yanagita into three stages: I: From 1923 to 1934: the formative period of the Yanagita school. He wrote such important books as Seinen to Gakumon (Youth and Study, 1928), A History of the Meiji-Taishō Period (1931), and A History of Japanese Agriculturalists (1931).

II: From 1935 to 1945: formation of the theoretical structure of the school. Minkan denshō-ron (On Oral Tradition, 1934), Kyōdo seikatsu no kenkyū-hō (A Method for Studying Rural Life, 1935), and other books were published one after another. In 1935, a nationwide organization called the Minkan-denshō no Kai (Association for Oral Tradition) was formed after a large-scale meeting among many local scholars who had contact with Yanagita and Shibusawa Keizō. The journal called Oral Tradition was started by this association.

Yanagita now began to carry out organized research on a nation-wide scale. His "Sanson-chōsa," and "Kaison-chōsa," large-scale research on mountain villages and oceanic (fishing) villages, respec-tively, were carried out in 1937. At the same time, a series of glossaries of local folk terms were compiled and published one by one. They finally comprised 17 volumes, including a couple put out posthumously:

1. Sanson (mountain village) glossary 1932
2. San'iku (childbirth and infantcare) glossary 1935
3. Sanson addenda 1935
4. Kon'in (marriage customs) 1937
5. Bunrui-Nōson-goi (farming villages) 1927
6. Sōso (funeral) 1937
7. Bunrui Gyoson Goi (fishing villages) 1938
8. Fukusō (clothes) 1938
9. Kinki (taboos) 1938
10. Kyojū (housing) 1939

11. Saiji (seasonal events) 1939
12. Bunrui-sanson goi (mountain villages) 1941
13. Zokusei (kinship) 1943
14. Bunrui-jidō-goi (children's terminology) 1949
15. Nihon Densetsu (Japanese folktales) 1950
16. Bunrui Saishi (rituals) 1964--posthumous
17. Bunrui Shokumotsu (food) 1964--posthumous

In addition to these, in 1955 at the age of 81 he published 5 volumes called Sōgō Nihon Minzoku Goi (General Glossary of Japanese Folkculture), which is a kind of re-compilation of the collections.

During the same period, Yanagita wrote many other important books. Nihon no Matsuri (The Festivals of Japan) in 1942, Kokushi to Minzokugaku (Japanese History and Folklore) in 1944, Shokumotsu to Shinzō (Food and Heart) in 1940, and so forth.

III. From 1946 to 1962 (his death), Yanagita contributed some other important and controversial books, such as Senzo no hanashi (About Our Ancestors) in 1946; the trilogy, Shin-kokugaku-dan (Essays in Neo-Nativism), which included Saijitsu-kō (Festival Days, 1946), Yamamiya-kō (Mountain Shrines, 1947) and Ujikami and Ujiko (Tutelary Deities and Their Believers, 1947); an ethnography based on a deceased disciple's sources, Kitakoura Minzokushi (An Ethnography of Kitakoura); and his final publication, Kaijō no michi (A Way Over the Sea) in 1961.

It seems to me that Yanagita's determination to establish "Japanese Folklore Studies" reached its height around 1935. In that year he celebrated his kanreki (60th anniversary of birth) with a large-scale seminar held at the Nihon Seinen Kan (Japan Youth Center) in Tokyo. The results were published by Iwanami Shoten under his editorship in the same year, and from them we can see what the meeting was like. Some, like Miyamoto Tsuneichi, met Yanagita for the first time at this meeting, although they had communicated previously. The people who gathered there became the core of an association called Minkan Denshō no Kai, Association for Oral Tradition, which became the central society of Japanese folklorists thereafter.

By this time, his purpose was clear: he aimed at the establishment of "Japanese Folklore" as an introspective study by Japanese themselves. This could be compared to the goals of some nationalistic thinkers in Europe, who looked for the origins, or a basis of identity, for the nationality to which they belonged. The best way to explain the concept of "Japanese Folklore Studies" is to use the German dichotomy of Volkskunde and Volkerkunde, the study of one's own national culture and the study of many cultures. The latter, of course is "ethnology," but the former, Volkskunde, is rather difficult to translate into English. It is certainly misleading if it is translated as "folklore," or "oral tradition." It is similar to "Canadian Studies" for Canadians, or "l'Etudes Quebecoirs" for Quebecoirs. Or, in some sense, it is comparable to "Black Studies" among blacks in North America.

Let me suggest another example. In Zaire since 1973, there has been a nationwide movement, or at least a propaganda campaign by the national government, to seek the "authentic Zairean," or "authenticité Zairois." There are more than 200 tribes and subtribes in the former Belgian Congo, and the dialects could total more than 300. The former colonial government did not make much of an effort at integration, and consequently independence in 1960 led to tragic internal wars with mercenaries and external interference. To integrate people, to achieve an integration on the national level, or to establish national institutions in many aspects of life, people have to seek a basis for integration of their culture into a national culture. All kinds of national symbols: flag, anthem, heroes, national sports, national language, and so forth, are for the sake of a common culture that can be shared by the people belonging to the country. This process is prerequisite to so-called "nation building," and might be called "the formation of a national culture." Countries like Zaire, and many others in Africa, Asia and Latin America, are now going through a painstaking process of the formation of such a national culture.

Japan was, of course, not an exception, although it had several advantages: a common language, a common cultural tradition, and a supposedly common ethnic background as a result of confinement to several islands for more than 200 years during the Tokugawa period (1600-1868). But even so, Japan had its own diversity: some 40 or 50 local concentrations maintained for several centuries, that resulted in distinctive local peculiarities. There had been four fixed classes, warriors, peasants, craftsmen and merchants, plus two sub-classes, the nobility and the outcasts, above and below these four social strata. Each had its own distinctive subculture, leading to considerable diversity that constituted an impediment to national integration. The Meiji Government was aware of these diverse elements, and by applying power from above, with police, schools, and local administration as the means of enforcement, tried to integrate them into a common national culture. The Meiji leaders created national symbols like the Emperor Meiji, drafted the constitution and the civil codes, and imposed other regulations. External affairs, including the Sino-Japanese and Russo-Japanese Wars, contributed to a tightening of this national integration.

However, this hasty process of integration into a modern national culture demanded vast sacrifices at the local level. Local dialects were mostly subject to insult; people who could not speak standard Japanese were treated as handicapped. Local traditions of marriage, kinship, community, and friendship, and also customs of trade, production, house construction, and so forth, were overwhelmed by elements of the new national culture. Folk beliefs and folkways, that is, were quickly replaced by new ideas that had been imported from advanced countries and integrated into the new national culture.

One can easily imagine that an "authentic Zairean culture" as such, does not exist because this is the name of a nation born only in 1973. It seems to me that there was a similar situation in Meiji Japan. The people had to create a national culture for Japan, too, even though Japan had more resources for that purpose than some countries, where there is not even a single candidate for a national language. But the difference is only a matter of degree. Japan went through its painstaking formation at the sacrifice of much local and subcultural diversity.

I think that Yanagita Kunio found precious survivals and valuable unwritten traditions that could form a part of Japan's national culture. So he intended to preserve them, by collecting from all over the country, and introducing them into national culture by presenting them in written, recorded forms.

10. His Achievement

If one examines Yanagita's life history carefully, one finds that his early concern for rural people in Japan gradually developed into a focus on survivals in the countryside, whether oral, mental or objective. He started conscious efforts to form "Japanese Folklore Studies" in the 1920s, and he substantially achieved his goal with the formation of a "school" in about 1935. Although Japan gradually fell under the shadow of militaristic chauvinism, he seems not to have suffered much from interference by military police or other harassment in the academic world. That is partly because he was already an established figure, with a glorious career that had led to his stint as secretary general of the House of Councilors. Also, he was cautious about expressing his ideas concerning Japanese folk belief when they would have contradicted the dogmas of the right wing.

Besides his poems, which have never been republished, he wrote more than a hundred books. Most of the major works are included in the 36 volumes of his collected works.

His writings cover a broad segment of the life and thought of Japanese. When I organized a taskforce with Dr. Itoh Kanji to analyze his works, we tentatively constructed the following classification:

1. His organizing activities:

   1910: Kyōdo-kai organized.
   1913: Journal "Kyōdo Kenkyū," editor (to 1917).
   1925: Journal "Minzoku," editor (to 1928).
   1933: Journal "Shima," editor (to 1934).
   1934: Research project on mountain villages.
   1935: Seminar on "Japanese Folklore Studies." Editor in chief of journal, "Minkan Denshō."
   1937: Research project on oceanic villages.
   1947: Research Institute for Folklore built (to 1957).
   1950: Research project on detached islands.

2. His literary activities:

   1897: An anthology, "Nobe no Yuki-ki"
   1925: Kainan Sho-ki
   1928: Yukiguni no Haru
   1932: Shufu-chō
   1958: Sumiyaki Nikki
   1959: Kokyo Nanajū-nen

3. His theories and hypotheses:

   1910: Jidai to Nōsei
   1928: Seinen to Gakumon
   1934: Minkan Denshō-ron
   1935: Kokushi to Minzokugaku
          Kyōdo Seikatsu no Kenkyū-ho
          Nihon Minzokugaku Kenkyū (ed.)
   1942: Nihon Minzokugaku Nyūmon (with Seki Keigo)
   1944: Kokushi to Minzokugaku (rev. ed.)
   1954: Nihonjin (ed.)
   1961: Kaijō no Michi

4. Life in village communities:

   1909: Nochi-no Karikotoba-no-ki
   1910: Toono Monogatari
   1926: Yama no Jinsei
   1929: Toshi to Nōson
   1931: Meiji-Taishō-shi Sesō-hen
          Nihon Nōmin-shi
   1939: Nōmen-izen no Koto
   1940: Shokumotsu to Shinzō
   1949: Kitakoura Minzokushi

5. Family, women and children:

   1929: Mukoiri-kō
   1932: Josei to Minkan Denshō
   1945: Mura to Gakudo
   1946: Ie Kandan

6. Ancestors and deities:

   1910: Shakujin Mondō
   1940: Imōto no Chikara
   1942: Nihon no Matsuri
   1943: Shintō to Minzokugaku
   1946: Senzo no Hanashi
   1947: Yamamiya-kō
         Ugigami to Ujiko

7. Oral literature:

   1932: Kōshō Bungei Taii
         Nihon no Densetsu
   1933: Momotarō no Tanjō
   1938: Mukashibanashi to Bungaku
   1940: Minyō Oboegaki
   1943: Mukashibanashi Oboegaki
   1946: Warai no Hongan
   1947: Kōshō Bungei-shi-kō
   1953: Fukō-naru Geijitsu

8. Language:

   1930: Kagyū-kō
   1936: Chimei no Kenkyū
   1939: Kokugo no Shōrai
   1946: Mainichi no Kotoba

9. Glossaries (mentioned above, p.)

In addition to these rather "scholarly" works, he published interesting text critiques of several poetry collections (rengashū), such as Sarumino, and wrote a number of short articles in Asahi shinbun and other newspapers and journals. The latter contain many insights and perspectives that are still provocative, particularly to those who are interested in Japanese cultural affairs, including cultural anthropologists.

As for his style of writing, I noticed that he often starts his writings in conjectural form. For example:

> For more than seventy years since my childhood we
> have wondered where the Japanese came from. . . .
> (Nihonjin, 1954)
>
> There is a question of whether or not matsuri and
> sairei are the same. . . . (Nihon no matsuri, 1942)
>
> The question which I would like to leave to the
> coming generation concerns not merely the small
> variations in tales of creation among the many
> people of the world, but, far more important for an
> understanding of early life in Japan, the problem of
> why and by what form of reason we began to call our
> giant creature daidarabō, or other similar terms.
> . . . (Daidarabō no ashiato).
>
> Does each person have a spirit? If so, where would
> it go after one dies? This is the first, biggest
> starting point. . . . (Watashi no tetsugaku, 1950)

This style of writing is effective in stimulating one's
curiosity about the ordinary things of life, and leading one to a
world of meanings that have long been forgotten on the surface of
ordinary life.

III. Some Evaluations

Mr. Itoh mentions in the postscript of his book on Yanagita
that he had decided to leave the world of Yanagita studies for a
while, and that decision had led him to write the book. I wrote almost the same thing in the introduction to our book, Yanagita Kunio
no setai (The World of Yanagita Kunio, 1976): "I would like to end my
comments on Yanagita now, and instead concentrate on the questions he
left for us. From the beginning of the work, we have attempted to
review his world as a whole."

Five years have passed since then, and I am now provided with a
chance to talk on Yanagita again, but in an entirely different environment. It took me by surprise, but now I feel grateful to those
who planned this workshop and gave me this opportunity. It has
allowed me to reconsider Yanagita and his heritage, in a different
setting.

About 13 years ago I sat on a panel of Africanists at an international conference of anthropologists. My paper was entitled "The Use of Japanese Anthropology in African Studies," and in it I explained that Yanagita Kunio had initiated the collection of oral traditions in modern Japan, and that Japanese experience in that effort might be useful to those countries that are trying to form their own national cultures. I think I emphasized that the tendency of traditional anthropologists to study peoples and cultures who are disappearing from the earth would not work for African leaders, who are, like Japanese in the Meiji Era, attempting to rid their people of traditional bonds and to forge for them a new nationality. It would be wise, therefore, to let them know the value of a non-literate tradition as a source of new national identity. We have the experience and know-how required to put oral tradition on the inventory of national culture and, in fact, many Japanese enjoy the results; having folk tales and traditions, originally from different parts of Japan, as his or her own property provides a person with a basis for identity as a Japanese, rather than as someone from Satsuma or Aizu. I do not think the other panelists (including Peter Gutkind, W. Goldschmidt, J. Macque, and others) were very impressed, because they have no such experience and needs. They can survive as cosmopolitan individuals who do not care much about identity or nationality. But for those Black Africans or Southeast Asians who are now looking for the means of nation building, the idea can be understood very easily. In fact, my research work on ethnoscience in Zaire during the 1970s was carried out with the cooperation of Zaireans who agreed with what I said. I feel like an exporter of Yanagita's ideas to Africa.

These ideas derive from my sympathy for those who are now attempting to lay the foundation for national identity in their own countries. Like the Meiji leaders, they must eliminate elements that disrupt nation building, and create their own sources of national identity in place of tribal, local or caste identities. I am very sympathetic to such leaders, who are more or less contemporaries of mine.

However, now that several years have passed I am beginning to realize some different aspects: I have seen the realities of nation building, and subsequently the formation of national-level culture. I have observed the conditions of minority nationalities in China; and while at McGill University, Montreal, I have seen what is going on in Canada. These experiences prevent me from offering simple, naive support to nation building itself. I realize that the formation of national culture is not a simple, optimistic thing. It causes lots of pain, tragedy, grief, and artificial distortions of people's lives and beliefs. I realize that success in creating one nation could mean the failure of another. The formation of a standard national culture could cause harm to many local cultures.

We have learned that "relativism" is the only possible attitude toward other cultures. Sometimes you must accept violations of your moral code, aesthetic taste, or other preferences when you observe another culture. I believe there is truth in all of them, but that makes for contradiction when there is a real clash of cultures.

Yanagita saved Japan's cultural heritage, especially as it inhered in "folk traditions." Such traditions are treasures not only of the Japanese but of mankind as a whole. If he had not preserved them, they might have disappeared from the earth. So in this sense we owe him a great deal.

At the same time, he had his own limitations. In trying to form "Japanese Folklore Studies" or "Volkskunde fur Japanischen," he tended to ignore relations with neighboring countries and peoples. The Kaijō no Michi, his attempt to trace the route of Japanese culture, is now considered almost totally mistaken, as Ryūkyū culture in fact developed later than Kyūshū. He had a lack of knowledge, or at least an unintentional ignorance, of Korean culture, which seems to be the closest and most important kin to Japanese culture. These handicaps derived from his own heritage of innate aristocratic and authoritarian behavior. It is a famous legend that he put on white socks (tabi) when he travelled, as if he were a feudal lord. He shunned any overt recording or discussion of the sexual aspects of Japanese life, which could have provided a rich source of insight into Japanese popular culture. He did not pay much attention to urban culture or even smalltown centers of local community (where he was born and raised), and he tended to treat cultural traits as separate items or particles rather than as aspects of a well-integrated cultural unit on the local level. He did not pay much attention to the need for ethnographies of various locales until he was 75 years old.

Yanagita Kunio was a well-read, clever, intellectual writer, who has given me great pleasure. He is always stimulating in some way or other, and constantly raises questions concerning our own lives. Nevertheless, I think it is now time to reassess his works.

PART II

INTERPRETIVE PERSPECTIVES

RITUAL AND 'UNCONSCIOUS TRADITION': A NOTE ON
YANAGITA KUNIO'S ABOUT OUR ANCESTORS

Yamashita Shinji

I will examine briefly Yanagita's conceptualization of Japanese ritual (matsuri), particularly the role of "unconsciousness" in the interpretations set forth in About Our Ancestors. First, however, we should be reminded of certain general considerations:

1) Folklore is for Yanagita not "a dead survival from ages past," as it was for European folklorists and anthropologists in the nineteenth century, but "a live, functioning part of the present-day world of man."[1] He repeatedly emphasized that Japanese society is noteworthy for the "liveness" of its folklore. He also stressed that the purpose of folklore studies is to answer questions about the present-day world, not about the ancients.[2] If he was interested at all in the past, it was to be the past within the present.

2) Concerning Yanagita's style of presentation, Hori and Ooms write, "the work (About Our Ancestors) shows characteristics both of the scientific report and the literary genre, much like the emaki (picture scroll) holds the middle between the tableau painting and the narrative strip."[3] The original title of the book indicates that it is to be less a treatise than a "talk" (hanashi) about ancestors.

1. A. Dundes, Interpreting Folklore (Bloomington and London: Indiana University Press, 1980).

2. Yanagita Kunio, "Gendai kagaku to iu koto," in Tsurumi Kazuko, ed., Yanagita Kunio shū (Tokyo: Chikuma Shobō, 1975).

3. Ichiro Hori and Herman Ooms, "Yanagita Kunio and 'About Our Ancestors'," in Fanny Hagin Meyer and Ishiwara Yasuyo, tr., About Our Ancestors--The Japanese Family System, by Yanagita Kunio (Tokyo: Japan Society for the Promotion of Science and Ministry of Education, 1970), p. 9.

So we might well read it as if we were listening to the stories told by our grandparents, not as a scholarly work.

3) It is also necessary to examine the work and thought of a scholar like Yanagita in relation to the time he lived. The motivations which guided his writing rose in response to trends and events of that time. Thus, About Our Ancestors, for instance, cannot be understood without reference to Japanese involvement in World War II.[4]

Keeping in mind these points, which I cannot discuss in detail in this paper, let us turn to problems of ritual and unconsciousness.

Yanagita's Conceptualization of Japanese Ritual

According to Yanagita, it is only through rituals, or matsuri, that we can appreciate the "authentic" form of Japanese religious belief and its historical transformation.[5] That is because Japanese belief is not essentially a religion of the "book," like Christianity, but a religion of practice, transmitted only through "action and feelings." Of course, over the centuries of Japanese history, there have been various attempts by intellectuals such as Shinto scholars or Buddhist priests to "authorize" or "rationalize" the dogmatic aspects of Japanese religious traditions. Yet, Yanagita argues that these have had nothing to do with the majority of Japanese folk, who live in a non-literate world. The following remark is illustrative:

> . . . it is rather fortunate that the sutra read at the altar was stale old Chinese, making sense neither to the dead nor the living, so they did not feel unhappy hearing it, for if they had understood its meaning in detail, they would have been startled.[6]

4. Ibid., pp. 4-5.

5. Yanagita Kunio, Nihon no matsuri in Teihon Yanagita Kunio shū, Vol. 10 (Tokyo: Chikuma Shobo, 1969). See partial translation in this volume, p. 167 ff.

6. Fanny Hagin Meyer and Ishiwara Yasuyo, tr., About Our Ancestors, p. 145.

In other words, the stress in Japanese folk religion has been, as Clifford Geertz observed with respect to Balinese religion, "on the orthopraxy, not orthodoxy--what is crucial is that ritual detail should be correct and in place."[7]

Yanagita established his perspective on Japanese religion in a book called Nihon no matsuri (The Festivals of Japan), published in 1941, five years before the publication of About Our Ancestors. The Festivals of Japan develops his analysis further in the field of senzo matsuri, rituals related to ancestors, while this time attacking Buddhist interpretations. The reason he attacked Buddhism is that Buddhism in Japan seems to have succeeded in penetrating Japanese notions related to death, the dead, and ancestors. In both works, which should be read together, his orientation (or bias) is toward anti-intellectualism, "authenticism," and nativism (kokugaku). In my view, that obvious value orientation does not detract from the merit of his works, but that will be controversial.

About Our Ancestors begins with a contrast between two interpretations of the word senzo (ancestor). One is favored by the intellectuals, or literate class; the other by illiterate, ordinary folk. According to the first, senzo is regarded as "one founder of the family . . . who lived and worked a long time ago." This interpretation retains the dictionary meaning of senzo, construing it "according to the way it is written." By the second, however, senzo is supposed to be "one who should be venerated" in the "live" context of a particular family.[8] Needless to say, it is the second interpretation with which Yanagita is concerned. Yet it seems to me that this choice requires some explanation, and unfortunately the translation does not convey the correct nuance of the original words.

The Japanese passage in question is: senzo wa matsurareru mono da, or ancestors are "matsurareru." The key word is matsurareru, the

7. Clifford Geertz, The Interpretation of Cultures (New York: Basic Books, 1973), p. 177.

8. Meyer and Ishiwara, tr., About Our Ancestors, p. 23.

passive form of the verb <u>matsuru</u>, which denotes "to hold a ritual."
Etymologically, as Yanagita argues in <u>The Festivals of Japan</u>, <u>matsuru</u>
comes from the same root as <u>matsurou</u>, which means "to be with (a
superior)" or "to serve (a superior)." So <u>matsuru</u>/<u>matsurou</u> is an
attitude in which one is happy to serve as a superior desires. Under
this root metaphor, <u>matsuri</u>, which is a noun form of <u>matsuru</u>, means a
ritual in which one experiences a "being with" or "serving of" deities
or ancestors. In this respect, we could add that the essence of Japanese ritual is <u>kami asobi</u>, "playing with the deities (or ancestors)."
Thus, we can now paraphrase the second interpretation: ancestors are,
first of all, the objects of ritual performance in the sense mentioned above. Furthermore, it might be interesting to note here that
Yanagita thinks the word <u>matsuru</u> was originally related closely with
the word <u>mairu</u>, meaning "to come (from the lower to the higher)."
(Even in contemporary Japanese, the word is used for "visiting" the
place of the superior in general, and especially for "visiting" a
shrine or grave.) In this sense, one <u>comes</u> to meet ancestors through
the rituals.

Against the background of these etymological considerations,
Yanagita postulates a Japanese "ancestor complex" (I prefer to avoid
the term "ancestor worship," which does not seem to me to fit Japanese reality) that focuses on the relationship between celebrators
(<u>shison</u>, or descendants) and the celebrated (<u>senzo</u>, or ancestors).
By this ritualistic interpretation, the relation between them is
direct because ritual is, after all, "experienced" or "lived."[9] And
in this "lived" ritual experience, ancestors come closer to the descendants: that is, the ancestors are <u>felt</u> as if they were "parents,"[10] or <u>jii</u>/<u>baa</u>, which means grandparents.[11] The essence of the
ritual, moreover, is very domestic: feeding. In both the reli-

---

9. S. B. Ortner, <u>Sherpas Through Their Rituals</u> (Cambridge:
Cambridge University Press, 1978), p. 5.

10. Meyer and Ishiwara, tr., <u>About Our Ancestors</u>, p. 65.

11. Ibid., pp. 136-38.

gious and secular domains, offering food is the primary way to establish and maintain a relationship. It is interesting that another
meaning of __matsuru__ is "to offer (from lower to higher)," especially
in the form of __tatematsuru__ (__tate__, in this case, being an emphatic
prefix), and that in antiquity politics was also referred to as
__matsurigoto__ (__matsuri__ matters).

     Thus, in ritual, ancestors are "lived" on the model of everyday
life, and through the ritual they are even "domesticated." It is
through the lense of ritual that Yanagita argues in several different
ways for the "familiarity of death":[12] that souls remain in their
local area after death instead of going far away, that there are frequent comings and goings between this world and the other,[13] and that
ancestors, or the souls of the dead, go to mountains or little hills,
from which they look down on the happiness of their descendants.[14]

Ritual and "Unconscious Tradition"

     In a sense, ritual is a synonym for the customs which one fol-
lows unconsciously. As Leach pointed out, through ritual acts people
__do__ something and simultaneously __say__ something.[15] However, from the
actors' point of view it is usually the case that people are not
necessarily conscious of the message they convey through ritual. At
least, there are various degrees of "depth" in consciousness. In
other words, one can perform a ritual act without knowing the meaning
of the ritual, just as one can speak a language without knowing the
grammar of that language. The following anecdote told by Hori Ichirō
(Yanagita's son-in-law and a folklorist dealing with Japanese popular
religion) is interesting on this point:

12. Ibid., chapter 64.

13. Ibid., pp. 145-46.

14. Ibid., chapter 66.

15. E. R. Leach, "Ritual," International Encyclopedia of the
Social Sciences, p. 523.

Hori: I don't believe in deities (kami) or the
souls of the dead. But I pay respect to the fact
that there are lots of people who believe in them.

Yanagita: (after a little thought) But you offer
tobacco to your dead father every morning, don't
you? What is it for?

Hori: Because I loved my father . . . and it has
been a sort of custom since my childhood. My
grandmother and mother made me do it.

Yanagita: That is evidence that you believe in the
souls of the dead. The Japanese belief system is
not a matter of logos, or reason (rikutsu), as the
European scholar explains.[16]

In this exchange, there exists an "unconscious" gap between
Hori's mind (disbelief in the soul) and his deed (ritual offering of
tobacco to the soul of his dead father). Hori seems to think it is
consciousness that determines belief or disbelief. In Yanagita's
view, on the other hand, it is the unconscious deed that reveals belief. According to the latter, the Japanese belief system cannot be
understood without searching for the unconscious tradition which lies
beneath customary behaviors. I am not sure if Hori was convinced by
this explanation. He would say, "Yes, it might be so, but . . ."
Indeed, we might have the same feeling after reading About Our Ancestors, regarding the equivalence of New Year and Bon, the alternation
between ta-no-kami and yama-no-kami, familiarity with death, and so
on. The reason for our hesitation is that his interpretation is concerned with "unconsciousness."

By the term "unconsciousness," I do not mean to imply the
Freudian notion of unconscious projection, nor a Jungian collective
unconscious. We are confronted rather with a general situation in
which an analytical model is constructed using conscious as well as

---

16. Cited in Sakurai Tokutarō, "Yanagita Kunio no sosenkan,"
in Tsurumi Kazuko, ed., Yanagita Kunio shū (Tokyo: Chikuma Shobō,
1975), p. 420. Free translation.

61

unconscious materials from the society studied.[17] Let me explore this further in the context of Yanagita's work.

1) Throughout Yanagita's works, etymology, or considerations of the dialects of Japanese in that connection, occupy a very important place in his interpretation of folklore. It seems to me that etymology and dialectology provide him with useful weapons with which to "revitalize" the authentic power of a word which over time has sunk into the deep, unconscious strata of people's minds. Through etymological reasonings of this sort, he tries to go beyond everyday semantics to the place where a word is "lived" in "authentic" contexts. The derivation of matsuri, mentioned above, is a good example.

In About Our Ancestors, the etymology of hotoke plays a strategic role. In ordinary usage, hotoke denotes "Buddha," and also the dead or the "soul of the dead," since Buddhism is associated with death in the ordinary Japanese way of thinking. Yet Yanagita argues that the word is derived from hokai or hotoki, a "vessel," which is used to carry or to offer food.[18] From this, he also thinks that the word Bon, for the Japanese ancestral festival in midsummer, which is usually assumed to be of Buddhist origin, originates from the word which indicates a "tray" (bon). In this way, he tries to place hotoke and bon in an authentic Japanese context, removing them from Buddhism, which is a religion imported from outside. That is, if the essence of Japanese ritual is offering food to spirits, the "vessel" on which food is offered could function as a metaphor of ritual performance itself. I am not sure whether this hypothesis is correct, because again it refers to processes beneath our consciousness. But whatever its ultimate legitimacy, the hypothesis itself helps us to see reality from a fresh angle.

17. Claude Levi-Strauss, Structural Anthropology (New York and London: Basic Books, 1963), pp. 281-82.

18. Meyer and Ishiwara, tr., About Our Ancestors, chapters 43-47, especially chapter 46.

2) In direct reference to an unconscious tradition, Yanagita writes:

> Through Buddhist influence, the Bon festival has clearly changed, but at present, due to its popularity and complexity, several old elements still remain preserved in it. The reason we pay attention to what was preserved among <u>old people, women and children</u>, aside from the explanations in books and reports from scholars, is that we search for the traces of old customs and <u>unconscious</u> tradition. Such unwritten, <u>fragmentary</u> materials have been rapidly vanishing in the wake of common school education. However, they were fortunately protected from outside disturbances because they looked so <u>trivial and rustic</u>. People born in villages think their customs are odd, peculiar to their own region. When they are <u>compared</u> with examples from other places, we realize for the first time that <u>they should not be looked upon as casual happenings in our cultural history</u>.[19] (emphasis added)

There are two problems here: a) Yanagita's attention to "old people, women and children" as carriers of "old customs and unconscious tradition," and b) the issue of his comparative method.

"Old people, women and children" have been minor, or marginal, elements in the social consciousness of Japan's modernization which, Yanagita thinks, began in the fifteenth century,[20] and has been accelerated since the Meiji era under the impact of the West. The reason for Yanagita's attention to them is that, because of their structurally inferior position in the society, they are the unconscious bearers of an authentic, Japanese tradition, totally without rationalization. To the modern social consciousness, what they preserve seems "trivial and rustic." Yanagita, however, thought that they were the "real" carriers of Japanese cultural tradition amongst the superficial "modern men" of Japan. From this point of view, he pays special attention to childrens' rhymes in which the ancestors

---

19. Ibid., p. 133.

20. Yanagita Kunio and Ienaga Saburō, "Nihon rekishi kandan," in <u>Yanagita Kunio taidan shū</u> (Tokyo: Chikuma Shobō, 1964), p. 188.

are referred to as "grandparents."[21] This metaphorical relationship between ancestors and little children seems to provide Yanagita with the central imagery of the Japanese ancestor complex: children learn unconsciously about their ancestors through the model of their living grandparents, while grandparents see the rebirth of ancestors in their grandchildren.[22] Bon, as well as New Year, is thus a happy occasion in which this unconscious transmission is achieved.

Ronald Morse has pointed out with respect to Yanagita that "he did not focus on any one person, village or region: his unit of analysis was Japan."[23] In other words, evidence from a single person, village or region is "compared" to that from other areas and digested into his scheme of Japanology. About Our Ancestors is a typical example of this sort of "comparative" approach. But we cannot deny our impression that the materials he draws from here and there are fragmentary, without sufficient consideration of context. It is natural, therefore, that this kind of approach has caused dissatisfaction among the younger folklorists in Japan, who emphasize a "contextual approach."[24] However, from Yanagita's point of view again, data that seem to be "fragmentary" are always destined to take their place as interdependent elements in his hypothetical "organic whole": a Japanese Culture. He was concerned not with a "mechanical model," the elements of which are "on the same scale as the phenomena,"[25] but a hypothetical model whose scale is different. The ultimate context in which he observes a fact is beyond the consciousness of any particular village. Here again, we are confronted with the problem of unconsciousness in relation to his "comparative

21. Meyer and Ishiwara, tr., About Our Ancestors, chapter 60.

22. Ibid., chapters 77-78.

23. Ronald Morse, "Personalities and Issues in Yanagita Kunio Studies," Japan Quarterly, Vol. 22, No. 3, p. 241.

24. Ibid., p. 252.

25. Levi-Strauss, Structural Anthropology, p. 283.

method," and it is relevant to cite here his statement that "(in Japan) in most cases, to reflect on oneself is to collect, to classify and to compare (folklore)"[26] (emphasis added). It is well known that Yanagita defines his folklore study as a discipline of self-reflection. From this perspective, comparison is a tool for unearthing one's unconscious self, and Yanagita's work begins to look very much like an "archaeology of the folk mind."

Conclusion

I have begun to examine expects of Yanagita's conceptualization of Japanese ritual and the importance of an unconscious tradition in his understanding of folklore. I would like to conclude by citing a most impressive but very difficult sentence from About Our Ancestors:

> That faith was not a matter of personal feeling but a common experience of many people, which has never been proved so clearly as through the present war.[27] (emphasis added)

Apart from its context, this statement seems to me to express the essence of Japanese religion. My rather free translation of the passage underlined would be: in Japan, "to believe" is not a matter of individual feeling, nor of personal achievement, but a moral entity which is experienced and transmitted unconsciously from generation to generation (in the original Japanese text: shinkō wa tada kojin no kantoku suru mono dewanakute, mushiro tasū no kyōdono jijitsu datta). This view of Japanese religion is deeply connected with the concept of keishin (respecting deities, not believing in them) which seems to be fundamental to an understanding of not only the Japanese belief system but social relationships as well. Unfortunately, an examination of this problem must be deferred to another occasion.

---

26. Yanagita Kunio, Minkan denshō-ron in Teihon Yanagita Kunio shū, Vol. 25 (Tokyo: Chikuma Shobo, 1970), p. 355.

27. Meyer and Ishiwara, tr., p. 145.

YANAGITA KUNIO'S "ABOUT OUR ANCESTORS":
IS IT A MODEL FOR AN INDIGENOUS SOCIAL SCIENCE?

Bernard Bernier

Yanagita Kunio is undoubtedly one of the most influential
Japanese intellectuals of the 20th century. The impact of his work
can still be felt very strongly in the general public and in academic
circles in Japan. Although very popular in his own country, Yanagita
has not had much appeal outside of his homeland, even among Western
"Japan experts." Is it that Westerners have not understood some
aspects of Japanese culture? Is it that Japan's unique character,
manifested in Yanagita's work, is really incomprehensible to Westerners? These questions, it seems, were important for the organi-
zers of the Yanagita Kunio workshop held at Cornell University in
April-May 1982. For when one of them asked me to participate in this
workshop, the question that was presented as the center of my possible participation was the following: can Yanagita's work be conceived as the basis of a genuine Japanese social science and possibly
as a model for non-Western ethnic anthropologies?

As discussions progressed, the nature of my participation became clearer. I was asked to participate with two or three other
anthropologists in a discussion on one of Yanagita's most important
books: Senzo no hanashi. The reason for the choice of this book was
that it had been translated in English under the title About Our Ancestors. This was meant to facilitate a discussion that was to include people with no knowledge of or variable competence in Japanese.
As it turned out, this choice was questioned during the workshop
because About Our Ancestors was described as "not one of Yanagita's
best books" and as "badly translated."

65

Also the peculiar character of the book was clearly underlined: it had been written in 1945, just before the end of the war, when Tokyo, where Yanagita was residing, was under heavy fire from the U.S. Air Force; because of that, Yanagita could not rely on his notes; he felt a sense of urgency about his task, that is, he wanted to write as fast as possible about various beliefs and practices so that people after the war would know about them. The deep sense of personal involvement that Yanagita felt when writing the book was presented at the workshop as a limitation to the analytical value of the book. However, bearing in mind the peculiar character of Senzo no hanashi, it is possible to find in it methodological and theoretical characteristics that are essential to Yanagita's mode of analysis. At least, that is what I gathered from a partial reading of two of his other books[1] and from the discussion at the workshop. If this is true, comments about Senzo no hanashi can at least partially apply to Yanagita's thought in general. At the least, judgments about this particular book can be seen as hypotheses on Yanagita's method and point of view that would have to be confronted by the rest of his work.

As for the translation, even though I have ·not read the whole Japanese original version, I have checked carefully all the quotes used in this text and I have found no discrepancy between the translation and the original.

The task I gave myself was to answer one question: does Senzo no hanashi stand as a (partial) analysis of Japanese society and religion and as a methodological and theoretical basis for a peculiar Japanese social science? I tackled this task with a precise point of view which I can characterize in the following ways. First, it is the point of view of a Westerner trained in social science, especially in anthropology. I consider my work as a very small part of this diverse and contradictory intellectual current that is called

---

1. Nihon no matsuri (Tokyo: Kōbundo, 1942), and Shinto to Minzokugaku (Tokyo: Chikuma, 1943).

"scientific" or "rational." This current was systematized mainly in the Western World with the advent of commercial and later industrial capitalism. The goal of scientific research is to grasp the functioning of the various levels of reality (physical, biological, socio-cultural, psychological etc.). The postulate here is that there is a reality outside the observer, a reality which functions whether the observer studies it or not. Conversely, the observer cannot possibly study a reality with a blank mind. He inevitably has a point of view which is determined historically, socially and personally. Because of that, "scientific" knowledge is always relative and partial. "Scientific" knowledge is ideological although its characteristics make it different from other forms of ideology. Also, scientific research can, in certain conditions, directly affect the object of study.

Second, I have done various types of research in Japan. Especially, I have done fieldwork on folk religion at the village level. This research is peculiarly relevant here since it dealt with many cultural and social aspects which are essential to Yanagita's work. My study of folk religion was done in a village of Kii peninsula, in the Kumano region. The name of the village is Sone, located in Owase-shi, Mie prefecture. For more than a year in 1967-68 and 1970, I did research on rituals and their significance in the context of the economic, political and social relations, and daily life, of the people of a fishing village of about 600 persons, in a remote mountainous region (Bernier, 1975). I have also done field work as well as extensive library work on agriculture (Bernier, 1980).

Third, I come from a region of the world, Quebec, where a strong nationalist movement has existed for a long time. This movement has resulted in a peculiar view of Quebec society as unique and not understandable by outsiders. The only true comprehension of Quebec, according to this view, is by participation, this being often reduced to the descendants of the original French settlers who came to Canada before 1760. Knowledge is reduced here to the level of affective or emotional elements. This attitude, actually, is not so different from that of Yanagita and his followers who think that only through a total affective participation in Japanese society can a genuine Japanese social science emerge. My own experience of a peculiar "ethnic" sentiment in Quebec will be of help below in my analysis of the "unique" character of Japanese society.

In assessing the importance of Senzo no hanashi as a possible model for social science, I will proceed in three steps. First, I will compare some of Yanagita's conclusions with the data I gathered in Sone on two series of subjects: a) the ancestors, the newly dead, obon and the after-life; b) the ujigami, rites of fertility, the village and the family. Second, I will examine some important methodological issues raised by Yanagita's book. Third, I will analyze a few basic theoretical points which are brought out by Yanagita's treatment of the material he uses.

1. Yanagita's Analysis and Folk Religion in Sone

a) The Ancestors, the Newly Dead, Obon and the After-life

One element that Yanagita insists upon and which has great importance in Sone is the distinction between the ancestors and the newly dead (see p. 85 sq.[2]). In Sone, however, contrary to what Yanagita found in many regions, the distinction only operates in the first year after death. This is peculiarly clear at obon, the soul festival held in August. During this festival, families in which a death occurred in the previous twelve months make an elaborate, temporary altar for the newly dead. This altar is a special one, located in the main room of the house but outside the butsudan (household ancestral altar). On it are put offerings of flowers, fruits and vegetables. All the other families in the village put the same products, but in much smaller quantities, in the household's butsudan as offerings to the ancestors.

----

2. All references are to the English edition. See Bibliography.

Another element of the <u>obon</u> celebration also marks the difference between the ancestors and the newly dead: whereas the ancestors
leave the village on August 15th, the newly dead leave in two stages,
on August 16th and 19th. Also, the ceremonies to ease the departure
of the newly dead are much more elaborate than for the ancestors. On
August 16, all villagers gather at the harbor. There a small wooden
boat about four feet long is ceremonially transferred to a fishing
boat. In the small boat are placed some of the offerings of the
elaborate altars as well as folded pieces of paper on which the names
of the newly dead are written. This small boat is then carried to
the sea, on the Black Current, in order to send it away. If it were
to come back to Sone, the villagers would be hurt by the newly dead.
On August 19, again at the harbor, all villagers gather to witness a
ritual whereby Chinese lanterns, each representing a person deceased
the previous year, are burned and the ashes swept into the sea. As
opposed to this, the ancestors are sent away on August 15 through a
small household ceremony called <u>okuribi</u>: "sending-away fire." This
ritual, performed by one of the members of the household, preferably
a male, consists of burning a few pine sticks in front of the main
door of the house.

Let us go back to the ceremony of August 16. There is implied
in it a conception of the after-world and of the relation between the
living and the dead. Obviously, as the return of the ancestors at
<u>obon</u> clearly shows, there is a close relation, a certain continuity,
between the living and the dead.[3] In fact, the dead are brought back
to partake in the living's joy. But for this relation to function
properly, it is essential that, as an initial step, the newly dead be
disposed of in the right fashion. The newly dead are considered
potentially dangerous before their first <u>obon</u>. To eliminate this
potential danger, the newly dead must be sent far away, at least

---

3. It is apparent also in the fact that ancestors are given
offerings at all important rituals. Also, they are informed of all
important events, mainly joyful ones, that affect the household
members.

once, at the time of the first <u>obon</u> after their death. Only if this is insured can these souls come back later at the festival of souls as part of the group of ancestors.

These practices in Sone do not fit with Yanagita's interpretation. According to the latter, rituals for sending the souls to far-away places, such as the boat festival in Sone, are not of indigenous origin because these rituals contradict the idea of continuity between life and death and between the living and the dead (p. 152 sq.). To Yanagita, since this idea is central in Japanese religion, such practices must have been imported from other countries. I cannot say whether the idea of sending away the newly dead is indigenous to Japan or not. However, it is clear that, in Sone, contrary to Yanagita's interpretation, people do not see a discrepancy between sending the souls of the newly dead to a far-away place across the sea, on the one hand, and, on the other, keeping a proper continuity between the living and the dead. Rather, the former is a necessary condition of the latter.

Perhaps, in this instance, Yanagita has applied to popular religion notions of congruence and contradiction that do not really matter to the common people. If this were true, Yanagita would have imposed on the data his own peculiar way of thinking. He would also have assumed a certain configuration of the pure Japanese religion that would not fit at least some data. Maybe Yanagita has defined a general pattern of Japanese religion that is too rigid to include the various rituals and beliefs present in Japan. From my own experience and reading, there seem to exist some general principles of Japanese religion that are common all over Japan (such as the beliefs in the <u>kami</u> and the ancestors) but the peculiar beliefs and rituals even in relation to these are really extremely varied. If this is accepted, then the rather monolithic view of Japanese religion that seems to permeate <u>Senzo no hanashi</u> would have to be modified (see R. J. Smith, 1974a and b). But more on that later.

b) The Ujigami, Fertility Rites, the Village and the Family

Yanagita asserts that kami in general and ujigami in particular
are ancestors that have been deified and forgotten as ancestors. In
their introduction to the English translation, Hori and Ooms (p. 6)
mildly criticize this assertion, saying that, if ancestors were so
important to the people, how come they were forgotten as such and
became kami?

Yanagita's position on this point is based on his conception of
the primary importance of the family and of kinship ties as the basis
of village communities and of the whole nation (see pp. 43, 56 and
178). One quotation is given to illustrate.

> That the country has continued for 3000 years and
> more gives some meaning to the fact that descendants
> have not died out. But if we only depend upon our
> memory in worshipping the ancestors, we cannot help
> feeling anxious about the unity of the single line
> of descent of our race. (p. 133)

The importance that Yanagita gives to the family in village
solidarity, illustrated through a careful analysis of branch families[4] (p. 28 sq.), is also manifest in his conception of the relation
between family ties, the ancestors and the rituals of prosperity.
For example, Yanagita writes thus on the reason why the Toshi gami
(The God of New Year) is thought by merchants to be a fortune god and
by farmers to be a field deity:

> One conception concerning this faith is that if this
> deity is worshipped each year, the family will pros-
> per, and this will be manifested especially in the
> good yield from the rice fields and the gardens of
> the family, the response of the previous years con-
> firming it, and for various families whose gain or
> loss does not follow, there may not be kami other
> than ancestral spirits who can be relied upon to
> protect and support each of them. (pp. 57-58)

Another more explicit passage:

---

4. Hori insists even more strongly on the importance of the
Dozoku (see Hori, 1968, pp. 49-81).

> If besides making a household prosperous and rice
> fields bear abundantly, even granting another year
> of life is due to the power of Toshigami, the iden-
> tification of this deity with family kami is quite
> clear. I can hardly think of any other deity that
> serves the family to that extent. (p. 59)

Two points stand out in these quotes: first, the reduction of
village and national life to descent; second, the equation of kami
and ancestors through the rites of prosperity. To examine each
point, I will give examples from Sone.

In Sone, there are no large kinship based organizations of the
dōzoku type. Indeed, as others have pointed out, this is not excep-
tional (see Beardsley et al., 1959, Chapter 10, especially pp. 265-
269; Befu, 1965, pp. 1334-37). In 1970, the 600-odd people in the
village had 26 surnames, at least 10 of them going back as far as the
18th century and at least 4 to earlier periods. The village itself
seems to have been inhabited continually for many centuries. Documents found in the village and dating to the 17th century do not
refer to any large kinship group. Indeed, all of these documents
rather support the existence of many small independent family units.
Thus, we have here an old village whose community organization
depends very little on kinship and where many families have early
roots. Despite this, village solidarity and the distinction from
neighboring villages are strong and were definitely stronger in
earlier years. The means to insure this village collective identity
were local history, peculiar rites, a miyaza and, of course, the
village shrine and the temple. Community relations were organized
around a common life and the joint but unequal management of forest
and sea resources. The high points of village collective identity
were two important rituals centering on the ujigami of the shrine:
the New Year's festival and the shrine festival in November. Kinship
ties had a minimal role in this community life.

In this context, Yanagita's hypothesis on the origin of a
single ujigami from many family deities is difficult to accept:

It is possible to investigate how these kami of a
number of clans became united. It might be better
to say that the festival itself, became united, for
while the festival was held on the same day and at
the same place, many people began gradually to think
the deity was the same. . . . Usually, the festival
site of the most influential family was used by
others. (pp. 126-127)

Besides being founded on few reliable facts, this hypothesis
simplifies human relations by postulating that community ties can
originate in or be founded only on kinship groups. As anthropologists know from studies of various parts of the world, kinship, although extremely important, is only one basis of social relations.
Contiguous residence, the sharing of the same environment, and political or military control are among the other bases of social relations. There are communities such as Sone in which kinship plays a
secondary role, but that nonetheless have solidarity on the basis of
their economic or political life. The reason is that human beings
are related to one another in various ways and by various means,
kinship being an important one, but only one of them.

Political unification of a territory and control of its population through military conquest is another way to force people into
relations. If the unification lasts long, it can result in the development of solidarity and a sense of participation among the
people. If the population is small, kinship ties can become one
major means to insure this solidarity. But in huge states where the
population is large, real kinship ties can hardly be used as the
chief cement of social relations. In Japan, despite the kokutai
ideology that defined Japan as a single line of descent, an ideology
which seemingly Yanagita took at face value, Japan and her people in
the 20th century (and before) cannot in any way be conceived as kinship units. It is interesting, and indeed it demands explanation,
that a kinship ideology was used. But in no way can a population now
totaling 118 million live together on the sole basis of kinship ties
nor can it descend from only one or indeed a few lines of descent.
Historical data on the unification of Japan from the 3rd to the 6th

century A.D. testify to the existence of independent cultural and political entities that had to be forcibly included in the expanding Yamato kingdom. (See, among others, Ikawa-Smith, 1979 and 1980.) I think we can correctly infer from these elements that there is a multitude of lines of descent in Japan from prehistoric times.

Yanagita's insistence on the family brings him, in fact, to an ignorance of various forms of human solidarity and community, some of which undeniably exist in Japan. Yanagita's view on this simplifies the variety of Japanese human relations.

Let us turn to the second point: the rites to insure prosperity. As we saw, Yanagita asserts that the deity these rites are directed to must be a family deity (or deities) since the social unit which profits from them (through bountiful harvests or fortune) is the family. This is an unacceptable conclusion. In all religions, Gods are supposed to give things to human beings; and these human beings are part of family groupings. Would this mean that all Gods are originally family deities since they bring advantages to families? There is here, again, a simplification of forms of human groupings and solidarity that leads to the merging of larger social ties into family relations.

But what about rites to insure prosperity in Sone? These rites are related chiefly to the shrine and they exclude contact with death and the ancestors. In fact, Sone religion is divided in two complementary but separate parts: one deals with life, prosperity, fertility, purity and is centered on the _ujigumi_, the other deals with death, the ancestors, impurity and is centered on the temple and the butsudan. Rites of life and fertility are part of a diffuse view of humanity and the universe whereby these are forces behind natural phenomena, forces that have to be honored at festivals in order for the universe to function properly. These forces are at the same time natural, that is, intrinsic to natural phenomena, and extra-natural in that they must be distinguished from purely organic processes. They are the _kami_. The link to natural phenomena can be direct, as

in the case of the Yama no kami (the deity of the mountain who in-
sures the growth of trees) or the kami of an old tree. It can also
be more general, as in the case of the ujigami who insure village
prosperity by promoting the growth of all natural products necessary
for survival. Some kami are not linked to natural phenomena, but
they can bring good luck or, less often, bad luck. In this case,
naturalism is less clear, although good luck or bad luck is thought
of as emanating from a correct or incorrect relation to the kami and
the universe.

The relation between the kami and the ancestors is complex.
Some ancestors, that is, some special persons that died long ago and
indeed all the old ancestors, become kami. For a dead human being to
become kami, it takes either special qualities, which are taken as a
sign of the kami nature of the person, or time, that is, many generations. In the first case, it can be said that it is a special extra-
natural force that gives them "divine" qualities. In the second,
time partially erases the impurity linked with death. One thing,
however, should be underlined. Neither of these types of kami are
honored at the shrine and indeed, no rites whatsoever are made
peculiarly for them. In fact, they must be kept strongly apart from
the shrine and the rites for them are held, as for all other ancestors, at the temple. Despite the fact that some dead persons, after
a long time, become kami, their kami nature is amorphous and is still
imperfect. It can be said that, in Sone, kami and ancestors are two
kinds of spirits that are exegetically and ritually kept apart. The
old ancestors that have become kami operate a conceptual link between
the humans and kami but only an imperfect one.

This distinction between kami and ancestors is the basis for
two distinctive sets of rituals that have their special elements and
meanings. One, centered on the shrine, has a very strong naturalistic flavor, not unlike the "animism" characteristic of other religions in Asia and elsewhere (see Hori, 1968, p. 5 sq., Earhart, 1969,
p. 5 and p. 10 sq.). Some scholars have indeed insisted on the

necessity to compare some aspects of Japanese kami beliefs with elements of popular animistic belief in Korea, China, Southeast Asia and elsewhere. Ancestor worship does not partake at all in this naturalistic conception of the world. Both naturalism and ancestor worship are part of Sone religion, but, even if they are seen as somewhat complementary, they are kept strictly apart. This, indeed, seems to be the case, in various degrees, in many villages in Japan.

Despite the current separation between kami beliefs and ancestor worship, could these two parts of Japanese religion have the same origin, as Yanagita argues? Are not the ujigami "deities of the clan"? Is it not true that the ancestors, even though they are strictly separate from the shrine, are asked to partake in family happiness during shrine festivals?

The answer to the first of these questions must be tentative. It is indeed possible that ancestor worship and kami belief had their source in the same original cult. Ariga adopts this position (Ariga, 1967, quoted in R. J. Smith, 1974b, pp. 8-9). He sees the ujigami as, probably, in its origin, the lineal ascendant of the head of the uji. The uji itself is conceived as having evolved from a localized kinship group to a political unit covering many of these groups. The constitution of this unit was probably through conquest. The leader of the unit could have imposed his own ujigami, that is, the deity of his clan, as the tutelary deity of the whole political unit. As a consequence, the ujigami would have gradually lost his link to descent and instead would have become attached to a territory or a community not strictly defined by kinship.

Yet, it is possible that Ariga has projected backwards in time the importance that kinship and descent have had in later Japanese history. In fact, other interpretations are as plausible. Here is one. The descent connotation of the term uji is well documented in the case of noble clans competing for power and attempting to hold their official position at the court in the 6th century (see Reischauer, 1937, p. 8 sq.; also Miller, 1974). In this context, the relation between uji and descent is clear, although all the members of one uji might have had only fictive common descent. It is important to note, however, that there was no ujigami related to these noble uji. Thus, it is possible that the term uji in ujigami bears no relation to the descent organization that characterized the nobility; also that the strong descent content of uji appeared only with the advent of a clan of nobles that needed descent as a means to protect some interests. If this were the case, uji might have referred originally to territorial groups based (partly) on kinship but not necessarily conceived as descent groups. It would have been only when conquest by one group against others had occurred and later when a dominant noble class had appeared that uji, gradually, would have acquired its strong descent content. In this line of interpretation, the absence of link between the ujigami and descent could be explained by the fact that descent had less importance in prehistoric times than in the historic period, that is after the advent of the nobility.

Of course, both interpretations are conjectural. One insists on the descent aspect of uji and thus supposes a close link between ujigami and ancestors. The other one underlines the fact that the ujigami in historic times are village deities and not clan gods; thus, it argues that the ujigami might have had little relation to descent; consequently, since descent might not have been that important, the ujigami and the ancestors could have had independent origins. There is, however, no way to know which is correct.

Second, whatever the origin of ancestor and kami beliefs, it is clear that, from long ago, a certain distinction has been made, at least in some regions of Japan, between the kami and the ancestors. In Sone, for example, the kami are limited to life and are part of a naturalistic view of the universe and humanity. The ancestors are linked to family continuity but also to impurity, and no naturalistic belief is attached to them. It is true that the ancestors are asked to participate in the living's joy, mainly during ritual periods, but this is done in the household, not at the shrine. It is a sign that the dead are still members of the household. But even then, they possess a certain impurity which excludes them from the shrine. Clearly, in Sone, the _ujigami_ and the ancestors are conceptualized as two different kinds of spirits. Whether or not _kami_ and the ancestors were originally the same, in many historical manifestations of Japanese religion, a clear distinction has been made between the two. This distinction as well as the parallel but different development of both sets of beliefs that has occurred in many Japanese regions are ignored by Yanagita. In fact, on the basis of elements found in some Japanese beliefs of the 20th century, Yanagita has postulated an "original" unitary Japanese religion that embodies the implicit principles of some religious practices of his time (see 2 below). In this way, he generalizes from partial practices to the totality of Japanese religion. He also projects back in the past principles that have appeared in the course of historical development. For example, the ancestor cult that he associates with _Kami_ belief "in the beginning" is conceptualized as a purer form of ancestor worship than the one existing in his time, but embodying some underlying principles that he thinks can be uncovered under existing practices. This is an unacceptable way to proceed. First, it takes personal or regional practices and establishes them as the Japanese religion. As R. J. Smith has shown for ancestor worship, there exists in Japan a very strong variation in beliefs and practices (R. J. Smith, 1974b). Second, contemporary rites and beliefs can hardly be taken without proof as bases for determining practices dating back many centuries.

This is particularly clear in Yanagita's conception of the Japanese family as linked to ancestor worship. To Yanagita, the household (ie.) system that characterized Japanese society in the Meiji period was the model of the Japanese household, although he thought that this system had weakened in comparison to earlier periods. In fact, what Yanagita took as _the_ Japanese system, dating back to the beginning of Japan "many thousands years ago," is the one of the Meiji period, based on the historical developments of

preceding era, especially the Edo period, and on the legal systemati-
zation of early Meiji. Therefore, it was the product of a long historical process. And despite this development, there were still some
regional variations. It is reasonable to think that the "original"
pre-Yamato family system was quite different from the one of the
Meiji period and more varied. Yanagita could conceivably be right
about the common origin of Kami belief and ancestor worship and about
their link to kinship groupings but he is definitely wrong in postulating a unitary Japanese religion and household system and in projecting these forms backward in time. This procedure, actually, is
characteristic of Yanagita's method, to which I now turn.

2. Methodological Issues

Yanagita's way of dealing with data is sometimes illuminating
but his demonstrations are very often weak. One aspect of his method
which has attracted attention deals with etymology. This, actually,
is a crucial methodological point in the study of Japanese folk belief. Very often, people who perform rites or ritual actions explain
the meaning of these through the words used to designate some ritual
element. In Sone, for example, the use of a plant called Sakaki in
shrine rituals is explained by its relation to another word, Sakaeru,
which means "to prosper."

But there is a difference between using the explanations people
give of their own ritual through what V. Turner had called "folk
etymologizing" (Turner, 1969, p. 11) and the type of etymological
conjecture that Yanagita resorts to. Yanagita's etymological explanations are very often based on his own interpretation of what a word
means rather than on facts. This is particularly clear in Yanagita's
interpretations of the origin of bon and hotoke (pp. 99-109). It is
undeniable that such a procedure can lead to important insights. But
it is also undeniable that it can lead to arbitrary or conjectural
conclusions. In fact, the insights produced in this way

must be verified empirically rather than being offered as conclusions.

The arbitrary and conjectural character of many of Yanagita's conclusions is also manifest in some passages which are meant to prove certain interpretations.

> If the senzo-matsuri in the past had been like that at the present, families would not have continued as long as they have, and people would not have appeared to work so hard for the continuance of their family. . . . (p. 63)

As a proof that obon was not imported from outside Japan:

> If our people's intentions and the decisions for their families and descendants had been so feeble as to be immediately changed and revised by foreign teachings, our country would not have been brought to its present unity. (p. 144).

In these two passages, the reasoning follows this path: 1. Some element (A) of the present situation would not exist if another element (B) was in the past as it is now; 2. This being so, the second element (B) must have been otherwise; 3. How this second element (B) was cannot really be proven but we can postulate it; 4. Therefore, this element (B) was the way we postulate. This way of reasoning is weak in two ways: first, one cannot postulate that a situation would not have existed if previous conditions had been the same as in the present; there is no proof that the causal link one sees between elements is really existent; second, to postulate is not to prove; in order to prove or disprove something, conclusions must be based on careful research.

Yanagita's way of proceeding in the two passages last quoted is not accidental. It is congruent with one basic tenet of his methodological posture: that is, his total identification with the object of study. It would be more appropriate to use a different formulation: Yanagita's total identification of the Japanese people with himself. What Yanagita sets out to do in Senzo no hanashi is to prove what he already believes. This, he half admits: "It may be that I approached it with a certain thought in mind" (p. 150). It is even clearer in another passage which, despite the fact that, in the text, it does not pertain to Yanagita himself but to the people in general, applies totally to Yanagita's way of proceeding: "The faith itself is the basis for evidence of many facts" (p. 140).

We are dealing here with crucial methodological problems that are present in any enquiry into a specific sector of social reality. Can (or must) the research identify or empathize with the object of study? What interference will his beliefs cause in his enquiry?

Must he try to understand the way people see their world from the inside or rather try to explain it as a "social fact"?

The questions just raised have to do with faith, comprehension and explanation. Briefly, I think there is, as far as enquiries into social reality are concerned, an essential difference between faith and comprehension. And I would argue that Yanagita's method, despite the fact that it has been presented as an attempt to comprehend people's beliefs from the inside rather than to logically explain them, is based on the selection of facts to prove what is already a deep belief. In short, I would argue that Yanagita's method is closer to theology than to social science. Let me explain.

Faith admits of absolute truths that cannot be disproved. Methodologically, a believer starts with the conclusions and uses facts, whatever they are, as proof of these conclusions. The best recent example of this way of reasoning is the creationists' rejection of all the data on evolution. Other more perennial examples would be christian theologians' treatment of the historical person of Jesus-Christ or Muslim Fundamentalists' conception of Mohammad as a human being: the assumptions being here that the former was God and the second a prophet giving the word of God. Faith, which is usually but not exclusively linked to religion, is based on the search for absolute knowledge. Two procedures are possible here: one is "dogmatism," characteristic of most Western religions, which takes a text or collection of writings as containing all the fundamental truth;

the other is "total participation" with another person or reality. I would argue that Yanagita's faith partakes of both although his dogmatism is not based on a sacred book but on his own elaborations of the true Japanese faith. I will examine this point more deeply in the next section.

"Comprehension" is an attempt to grasp people's views as they are in order to reach their conception of the world and their perception of their environment. Here, the "truth" of the conceptions, in the sense that they adequately explain the world, is irrelevant. What matters is simply that they exist. They are socio-cultural facts and as such they are objects of study. What "comprehension" is about is an attempt to grasp at people's ideas as they live them. This attempt, of course, is always relative: we can approximate what people feel but it is impossible to participate totally in other people's views.

Explanation, which is often opposed to comprehension, is also relative. It deals with phenomena from the outside, trying to find relations of causality, congruence, logic or covariation between phenomena. Whereas, in comprehension, one cannot totally participate in other people's views, in explanation, one cannot really be totally outside the reality one studies. To my mind, explanation and comprehension must not be opposed. Rather, I see them as complementary. And indeed, I would argue that the main original trait of anthropology as a "scientific" endeavor has been a combination of both in order to achieve a more complete grasp of social and cultural phenomena. Of course, social scientists that are not anthropologists have tried to do the same and many anthropologists favor one to the exclusion of the other. What I want to underline here is that it is important not to discard either explanation or comprehension from our research procedures.

One thing that should not be forgotten when we attempt to comprehend social reality is that we do not approach this reality with an empty mind. This does not mean that we are necessarily always projecting our views on the reality studied. In order to avoid that pitfall, though, it is necessary to observe a few rules. One is that we should analyze a social reality with an open mind, not prejudging the conclusions before the research is done. Another is that we should treat cultural and social configurations as historical phenomena, that is, as situated in time and space. This means that we must relate the configurations we are trying to grasp from the inside to the social, economic, political, ideological and cultural context in which they originated or functioned.

I have made a distinction between the scientific method, based on a combination of comprehension and explanation, and the theological method. This does not mean that the former is perfect. As we all know, it has and always will have flaws. It cannot in any way generate absolute truths. But I would argue that, for the purpose Yanagita had in his own research, that is, to get at the facts about Japanese religion, the scientific method would have been much preferable to the theological one. And indeed, the selection of cultural facts out of context in order to prove a point, conjectural reasoning, and the reference to a true and pure original Japanese religion (see below), three elements that are fundamental in Yanagita's procedure in *Senzo no hanashi*, are characteristic of a theological way of thinking. This does not mean that all research done in a theological frame of mind is wrong or useless. On the contrary, many important elements can be uncovered and explained through it. The problem with it, though, is that these are interpreted in a context which is taken as absolute and unchallengeable and often with final conclusions already established.

3. Theoretical Issues

Yanagita's theological procedure, based on faith, has theoretical implications. One bears on the unique character of Japanese society and culture. This uniqueness is admissible within a certain context. In fact, all social units have their peculiar history, leading to specific social and cultural configurations. Contrary to a recent popular academic view on Orientalism (see Said, 1978), recognizing differences in social ways and in cultural systems is scientifically acceptable, and indeed unavoidable, and it does not automatically lead to discrimination. After all, people do behave differently in different societies.

What Yanagita does, however, is something else. First, he defines Japan as a socio-cultural entity that is totally and essentially different from the rest of humanity; second, he supposes that this entity has existed as such for "thousands of years."

Japan's uniqueness is not at all questioned if we recognize that some elements of her social relations and culture are shared with other societies, mainly the ones that are geographically the closest. Nor is it negated by the recognition that many social and cultural elements now present in Japan came from other countries. To believe that this recognition negates Japan's uniqueness, as Yanagita seems to do (see p. 144), can be based only on the conception of Japan as an entity so different from all other human societies that it cannot share anything with any of them. Without going so far, Yanagita's rejection of the Chinese, Korean or Indian origins of many religious elements now present in Japan is due to a very exclusivist conception of Japanese society. This conception is also to blame for his neglect of comparison of similar elements in Japanese, Chinese, Korean or South-East Asian folk religions. Uniqueness can never mean an absolute difference of essence. It refers to a peculiar social and cultural development in a specific historical and geographical setting by human beings whose innate functioning is similar to that of other human beings. There is a shared core that permits communication across cultural borders.

With this last position, it is easy to admit to uniqueness. But it is also easy to recognize shared or borrowed elements. It also permits one to adopt a point of view whereby it becomes possible, with hard work, to understand what other people believe or

think. This, of course, contradicts the position of many Japanese
(or many nationalists all over the world) who think that their culture is not understandable by outsiders. What is curious here is
that many of the Japanese who adopt such a position think they know
all about Western culture, philosophy or religion and make judgments
about them.

Yanagita's implicit position on cultural uniqueness is related
to his conception of Japan as a social unit dating back many thousands of years and based on one descent line. This position, which
is mythical and anti-historical, was standard belief in the ideology
of the 1889-1945 period. But it has been rightly questioned by historians before and after World War II. As we know from historical
and archeological studies, the unity of Japan as a country is a historical product. In this view, the Japanese nation did not appear
full-fledged once and continue thereafter but was constructed in
stages, with periods of strong decentralization. Although archeolo-
gists do not agree on a date, the earliest one proposed for the first
unification of the country (but excluding Tohoku, Hokkaido and the
South of Kyūshū at the time) is the 4th century. But a more plausible date might be the 6th century (see Ikawa-Smith, 1979 and 1980).
Thereafter, political centralization and territorial extension has
varied. It is not clear when people living on the islands that became Japan started to think of themselves as one people but it is
doubtful it predates the unification under the Yamato state. Before
that, there were many local tribes and kingdoms that have shared some
cultural elements (pottery, for example) but who were probably very
different in culture, social relations and language. But whatever
date is chosen as the start of a unified state and thus of Japan,
Japanese society, like all others, was constructed little by little,
to become what we know of it now. Admittedly, its identification as
"Japanese" originated many centuries ago. But nonetheless, it is not
an essence that appeared as a unique totality, completely and abso-
lutely different from anything else, and continued unchanging for

thousands of years. Japan has been and still is subject to historical process, like any other part of the world.

One could argue that Yanagita was aware of historical process,
as many passages of Senzo no hanashi might testify (see pp. 20, 32-
33, 61, 63 etc.). This is true, but in a very limited way. In fact,
contrary to what is written in Hori and Ooms's presentation (p. 8),
the conception of history which is implicit in the book is not really
evolutionary. Rather, I would argue that it bears more resemblance
to a type of theological thought current in many religions, especially in christianity, whereby the world or society are thought to
have degenerated from a pure, perfect Pristine state. A few quotes
from Senzo no hanashi will serve as illustrations:

> The difference between the KAMI and MITAMA altars
> suggests to us that there was once a far purer
> expression of faith than at present. (p. 124)
>
> It was largely due to the base activities of necro-
> mancers, and besides, it was because the faith in
> the kami of each family was weakened and lost power
> to overcome the uneasiness about calamities, just as
> in social life, the looseness of the tie to the clan
> led social intercourse to be inclined to flattery.
> (p. 164)[5]
>
> In our natural native religion, the pure theory
> which was accepted in primitive conditions still
> continues to exist (p. 170), but only unconsciously
> in far away places. (B.B)

This tendency to judge the present as somewhat degraded when
compared to a purer past is also evidenced through judgments Yanagita
makes about existing practices, and reforms he proposes so that actual religious beliefs conform to the purer state.

---

5. Just a parenthetical comment on Yanagita's opinion on
women: Yanagita asserts that men were not inclined to believe in
necromancers, implying thereby that women were (p. 165). Also, Yanagita writes that stories about ghosts tell about womanish, worthless
and personal matters (p. 167). Finally, about a woman who wanted to
be reborn in order to help her descendants, he writes that it was
courageous for a woman and a Buddhist (p. 177).

. . . it was wrong to have forgotten that there was
such a faith (p. 121)

When I asked why such a sacrilegious thing had been
done . . . (p. 121)

. . . its use at the present in various regions
would have to be revised. (p. 121)

Casting off the dread of death as soon as possible,
people long ago wanted to stand before the soul of
the departed with a pure, quiet heart, but this
feeling is becoming difficult for modern people to
understand. (p. 131)

But if we only depend upon our memory in worshipping
our ancestors, we can not help feeling anxious about
the unity of the single line of descent of our race.
We can not say that Buddhism disregarded this, but
when we look at how BON rites at the grave are celebrated, we can criticize it for not attaching more
importance in that direction. (p. 133)

What is implicit in these two groups of quotations is that, at
the beginning, there was a pure national religion which, unfortunately, mainly through Buddhism, has been adulterated. Fortunately,
the basic tenets of this religion, although mixed with "sacrilegious"
elements, are still visible, especially in the "natural" religion of
simple-hearted people. Yanagita's self-defined goal, at least in
Senzo no hanashi, is to uncover this purer national religion so that
people, if they wish it, could go back to original religious practices that are implicitly taken as superior to the present ones.
There is thus implied a degenerescence from a pure, original form.
This type of conception, interestingly enough, is present in the
works of many theologians of various creeds, when they feel that the
supernatural or the natural and social order has disappeared or is in
the process of disappearing.

One last theoretical point which is important in Senzo no
hanashi is the total ignorance of social inequality. This, it seems,
is a deliberate position taken by Yanagita in order to emphasize the
unity of all Japanese and the common Pristine culture they all share.

This position is made clear in Yanagita's use of the term jōmin ("ordinary people") to refer to all Japanese. To me, there is a problem here. For while it is important to refer to the common cultural elements shared by the Japanese, it is no less important to identify the social cleavages that are present in Japanese society. And these cleavages are not primarily "analytical categories" in the sense that they are imposed on the reality people live; very often they were perceived by the people or formalized in official theory or law codes. To give a few examples: the four-class system established by the Tokugawa in the 17th century identified four groups defined by their status and insisted on major cleavages, first between the nobility, the daimyo and the rest of society, second, between the samurai and the common people. This was official doctrine. In this context, it is surprising to find in Senzo no hanashi the following passage:

> In earlier times men in the upper rank of governmental service held land, and even if they did not dig and weed, that they lived on the profit of their land made them like farmers. (p. 41)

Obviously, in this passage, Yanagita chose to ignore a reality that was recognized by everybody at the time: that the lords and warriors were considered essentially different from farmers.

Another reality which Yanagita ignores is the difficult situation the tenants found themselves in between the end of the Edo period to roughly the beginning of World War II.

> . . . even a tenant farmer who paid the usual land tax could feel easy about food and clothing if he were willing enough to work . . . (p. 34)[6]

---

6. Yanagita's position here can be related to the paternalistic ideology stressing work as the sole factor of success, an ideology that was prevalent among management and government circles in the 20's and 30's and which was used to insure that workers worked hard for low wages. (See Marshall, 1967, p. 97, quoted in Cole, 1979, pp. 229-230.)

There is much insensitivity to the impossible situation of the tenants in this sentence written by a man who was supposed to be sympathetic to "ordinary people." One could object that identifying the tenants as a class results in the imposition of analytical categories on people who do not conceive of reality in the same way. My answer to that is the following: the repeated efforts by the tenants to organize and resist expropriation and high rents are evidence enough of the importance of perceived class differences in the people's conception of their reality.

One last example: Cole, in his analysis of the origins of the nenkō system of employment in Japan, describes the relations in the work place at the beginning of the period of industrialization in Japan (about 1878) in the following manner:

> Prior to the adoption of the permanent employment practice, the dominant cultural symbols emphasized the individual employee's relationship to his work superior, who was commonly a master craftsman, a labor contractor, or a subcontractor. Such relationships were highly authoritarian and drew on those symbols associated with the superior-subordinate relationships of the feudal period. . . . What has come to be called management familism (. . .) had been, prior to the Russo-Japanese War (1904-5), more of an autocratic ideology emphasizing a master-servant relationship between employer and employee. (Cole, 1979, p. 14. Emphasis on certain words is mine.)

These three examples show how social inequalities were formalized, consciously used and/or perceived by various segments or classes of the society. On this basis,[7] I would argue that it is as important to analyze these inequalities as it is to emphasize Japan's unity. Indeed, it could be argued that this unity and Japanese culture as we know it is the product, at least in part, of class domination. As I mentioned earlier, the unification of Japan was imposed

_____
7. I would also argue that, even if they were not perceived by the actors, inequalities of power or of access to resources have to be taken into account in the analysis of any society where they exist.

militarily by a class of warriors on the common people. Furthermore, noble culture of the Heian period and _samurai_ customs of the seven centuries before Meiji (1868) have become the basis of much that is now considered Japanese culture. Anybody who has read on these periods of Japanese history knows that the nobles and the warriors considered themselves to be essentially superior to peasants or urban merchants, craftsmen and journeymen.

One could argue that the inequalities present from the 7th century on were copied from China and, through Buddhist influence, are really outside elements that were only superimposed on a basic egalitarian Japanese tradition. Without denying a strong egalitarian element in some segments of Japanese tradition, I would argue, on the basis of archaeological data, that social inequality existed in Japan many centuries before the introduction of Buddhism. Ikawa-Smith argues that the first signs of social inequality in Japan date from the middle of the Yayoi period (Ikawa-Smith, 1979, p. 25; 1980, pp. 143-144). This means that, in the 1st century A.D., some five and a half centuries before the advent of Buddhism in Japan, inequalities were already present. This, with the fact that Japan itself was a creation of military control over territory and common people by a class of warriors, is enough to force us to include inequality in our treatment of Japanese culture and society. Conversely, I would argue that the conclusions of any study, including Yanagita's, that ignores class, social inequalities, and history should be treated with suspicion.

Conclusion

As I have tried to show _Senzo no hanashi_ is based on some highly questionable principles, both methodologically and theoretically. I have singled out the following flaws: conjecture; absence of proven relation between facts and conclusions; an acceptance of fundamental truths that are seen as unquestionable and that therefore must be upheld whatever the facts; an ignorance of class, inequalities and history; and finally, a belief in the essential uniqueness of Japanese culture, based on the total uniqueness of the Japanese people. Because of these, the book cannot be taken in any way as a model for a specifically Japanese social science. I would argue, moreover, that the data presented in it must be used with extreme caution. That Yanagita had interesting insights into Japanese culture is undeniable, but these must be checked further through careful empirical studies.

This is not meant to deny any value to the work. Indeed, it is a very emotional testimony of an important Japanese intellectual. The feelings that are manifested in it must be respected. However, Senzo no hanashi can be taken neither as a model for social science nor as a work of major theoretical or even empirical import. It is data for the intellectual historian, in the same way that essays, novels or other works are. Given the importance of Yanagita as the creator of folklore studies in Japan and as an influential intellectual, special care should be taken by intellectual historians to examine his work. But in no way can it be taken to be very useful in establishing a strong social science. In reality, Senzo no hanashi is the non-systematic work of a conservative, nationalistic, religious intellectual who, in troubled times, is trying to revive an idealized (and largely fictive) ancient social and religious order.

Two questions remain: how are we to explain Yanagita's popularity among Japanese intellectuals? Is this popularity a guarantee that Yanagita's conclusions have some validity? My answer to the first question is only tentative: in fact, it is a problem for intellectual historians or for social scientists dealing more directly with current intellectual trends. I would argue nonetheless that the answer is to be found in the present international conjuncture whereby Japan, after nearly three decades of borrowing from the West, emerged in the 70's as the most economically successful nation in the world. This reversal of situation was bound to have some theoretical repercussions. One that has been evident in the West, mainly through recent books by Vogel (1979) and Ouchi (1981), is the attempt to import into America Japanese techniques of personnel management. To my mind, the attempt by Japanese scholars to question Western science and to look for Japanese models of analysis is another one. Since Japan is so good economically, why would Japanese not be equally good theoretically or methodologically? In this frame of mind, Yanagita was a likely candidate to be established as a model: he founded a "new" science, he never quotes Western scholars, he deals with only Japan, and he insists on the unique character of Japanese institutions. Given the resurgence of self-confidence and indeed of nationalism in Japan, Yanagita's popularity is not surprising. Another element in this remarkable rebirth of Yanagita's influence was mentioned at the workshop: it is the nostalgia urban Japanese feel for their roots in rural Japan.

Let us turn finally to the second question. To me, Yanagita's popularity among intellectuals in Japan is not a guarantee that his conclusions are right or even that his work is important as an analysis of Japanese society. Yanagita's appeal, as it appeared clearly at the workshop, is emotional. His way of writing, his personal feelings, appeal to the Japanese reader. But an emotional appeal can never be proof of the validity of any conclusion on a society. Human beings, including intellectuals, have been known to forget their critical judgment when an emotional appeal is made to them. One fairly recent and rather disquieting example is the overwhelming support of the German intellectuals for Nazism. Theories of racial uniqueness and superiority have a way of attracting people, including intellectuals, even though they are clearly unacceptable. These theories strike an emotional cord within people, but this does not mean that they are either true or useful.

Of course, social science is also caught in the close links among symbolic systems, emotions, political cleavages and economic conjecture. Science is not and will never be absolute knowledge. But there are some precepts of scientific research which, to me, remain basic: do not trust your gut feelings, be critical of every set belief, including your own, see your own knowledge as relative both in time and space. There is, of course, no guarantee that these principles will be applied, but they seem to me to be more fruitful and less dangerous than affirmations of total truth or comprehension through emotional participation or dogmatism.

BIBLIOGRAPHY

BEARDSLEY, Richard K., John W. Hall & Robert E. Ward, Village Japan.
1959   Chicago, University of Chicago Press.

BEFU, Harumi, "Patrilineal Descent and Personal Kindred in Japan," in
1963   American Anthropologist, 65.6, pp. 1328-1341.

BERNIER, Bernard, Breaking the Cosmic Circle: Folk Religion in a
1975   Japanese Village, Ithaca, N.Y., Cornell University East
          Asia Papers, no. 5.

_____, "The Japanese Peasantry and Economic Growth Since the Land
1980   Reform of 1946-47," in Bulletin of Concerned Asian
          Scholars, 12.1, pp. 40-52.

COLE, Robert E., Work, Mobility and Participation, Berkeley and Los
1979   Angeles, University of California Press.

EARHART, H. Byron, Japanese Religion: Unity and Diversity, Belmont,
1969   Calif., Dickerson Publishing.

HORI, Ichirō, Minkan Shinkō, Tokyo, Iwanami Shoten (1968 edition).
1951

_____, Folk Religion in Japan (Edited by Joseph M. Kitagawa and
1968   Alan L. Miller), Chicago, Chicago University Press.

IKAWA-SMITH, Fumiko, L'évolution politique du Japon à la fin de la
1979   période préhistorique, in Anthropologie et sociétés, 3.3,
          pp. 21-33.

_____, "Current Issues in Japanese Archaeology," in American
1980   Scientist, 68.2, pp. 134-145.

MARSHALL, Byron, Capitalism and Nationalism in Prewar Japan, Stan-
1967   ford University Press.

MILLER, Richard J., Ancient Japanese Nobility, Berkeley and Los
1974   Angeles, University of California Press.

REISCHAUER, Robert K., Early Japanese History (ca 40 BC-AD 1167),
1937   Gloucester, Mass., Peter Smith (1967 edition).

SAID, Edward M., Orientalism, New York, Pantheon.
1978

SMITH, R. J., Afterword, in Wolf, Arthur P. (ed.) Religion and Ritual
1974a   in Chinese Society, Stanford, Stanford University Press,
          pp. 337-348.

_____, Ancestor Worship in Contemporary Japan, Stanford, Stanford
1974b   University Press.

VOGEL, Ezra F., Japan as Number One, Cambridge, Mass., Harvard Uni-
1979   versity Press.

YANAGITA KUNIO, Nihon No Matsuri, Tokyo, Kyōbundo.
1942

_____, Shintō To Minzokugaku, Tokyo, Meisedo.
1943

_____, Senzo No Hanashi, Tokyo, Chikuma Shobō (Yanagita Kunio Shū,
1945   Vol. 10, p. 1969).
           Translation: About Our Ancestors, Tokyo, Japan Society for
           the Promotion of Science, 1970.

OUCHI, William G., Theory Z, New York, Addison-Wesley.
1981

JAPANESE SENSIBILITY: AN "IMITATION" OF YANAGITA

Tada Michitaro

Upon their first meeting in Japan, Amatsukami, the god of the sea and the heavens, found Kunitsukami, the god of the land and the country, very interesting. Amatsukami, who was foreign to Japan, posed a series of scientific, systematic questions to Kunitsukami, who was native to Japan. But Kunitsukami did not answer and remained silent.

* * * * * *

In the 1950's, a professor of the law faculty of Tokyo University, using the appropriate dialect, conducted a series of interviews with peasants in northern Japan to determine what remnants of obligation to feudal lords existed. Overwhelmingly, by 85 percent, the peasants reported that they felt no obligation to their landlords; only some 5 to 7 percent indicated yes, they did feel such an obligation. From this accumulation of scientific data, then, this professor concluded that Japanese peasants had made the transition to a modernized society, having thrown off allegiance to their landlords.

Such reasoning, however, is specious. What the professor failed to take into account was, first, that few people including himself, would choose to acknowledge their slavery to anyone, and second, that at festival times of the year peasants customarily present gifts to their landlords—this despite their claim to feel no obligation. It would seem that some observation by the professor, as opposed to the scientific inquiry he attempted, would have been the wiser methodology for his study. Even though observation would have been more desirable, it might yet have turned up misleading "facts,"

97

for, like social scientific questions, it would have been an imposition of a concept on a phenomenon. The result might distort the
"truth" to a lesser degree, but it would be a distortion nonetheless.

In tradition and ritual, true feelings are hidden; they lie in
a shadow and are indiscernible and unknown to anyone unless that person places himself in a situation by which he can share such an experience. The deeper truth of Kunitsukami's non-response to the
scientific questions of Amatsukami thus becomes quite understandable:
If Kunitsukami had tried to answer Amatsukami's questions, he would
have fallen into the framework of the questions, and this framework
was not only inappropriate but also irreconcilable to the phenomenon.
Silence, in the case of Kunitsukami, was the only possible response.

It is important, therefore, that there be no predetermined
method for inquiry into habits--national or otherwise. One must seek
instead to discern some kind of cultural code by which to connect to
the more obvious symbols in a culture. A poem, for example, can express an experience which both the poet and his audience create. In
this, no perceptual framework of scientific knowledge is imposed onto
the experience; whatever understanding that may be gleaned, thus,
occurs within the context of the experience. Instead of imposition,
there is an evocation.

Noh drama provides a quick example of such evocation. The
voice of our ancestors is given sound by the refrain of the chorus;
and the happiness of a moment is experienced in a dance with the gods
which can only occur in the shade of a pine tree. Hidden, subliminal, traditional feelings are evoked, and the experience becomes a
shared one. Proust evokes a similar kind of shared experience in
Remembrance of Things Past when he writes of eating the madeleine
with his tea. Not all of us have had an experience like Proust's,
but all of us have comparable experiences in which a certain smell,
taste, or touch generates a world of memories of childhood, tradition, ritual, or pleasure.

A cultural code that affords us a glimpse of habit and tradition, thus, concentrates not on the large major events of a time but rather, like Proust's madeleine, on small, ostensibly insignificant details and experiences. Accordingly, it is not the big symbols that are important, but the small; not the adult, but the child; not the elite, but the mass; not the center, but the periphery; not the ritual, but the play; not the light, but the shadow.

There are several examples of what I mean by this. First, in the small stalls that sell various goods in front of Shinto shrines at night, one can purchase the very popular masks of a clown called Hyottoko. (These masks, it is important to note, are not available in large department stores.) The face of the clown Hyottoko is contorted humorously into a mug: the nose is wrinkled, the mouth twisted, the eyes are squinting. Why the mug? According to Origuchi Shinobu, a contemporary of Professor Yanagita, Hyottoko descends from the prototypical clown Beshimi, which in Chinese characters, refers to illness. The popular belief is that Hyottoko's expression is the result of illness, but this idea, says Origuchi, is too easy, too pat. Instead, Origuchi suggests that the appeal and popularity of Hyottoko and Beshimi have more to do with Kunitsukami and the preference to remain silent in the face of unwelcome circumstances. By pursing his lips tightly together, choosing not to answer questions, Beshimi is the image of the clown Hyottoko.

In Western terms, however, the choice of silence made by Kunitsukami and Beshimi--that is, their choice not to respond--is construed as an act of irresponsibility. But again, there is more here than meets the eye: Friday gave no answer to Robinson Crusoe's questions of technology on the island, even as Caliban lacked the vocabulary to respond to the civilization of Prospero. Similarly, the apparent irresponsibility of Beshimi and Kunitsukami can be seen as the only reasonable response under comparable circumstances. The ethic of response is fundamental to the West, to "stronger" cultures. But if one is less strong, if one is "weaker," the ethic is less appropriate.

Irresponsibility, however, is not a universal virtue. As Japan has currently grown into a worldwide economic power, for it to remain silent becomes unreasonable. In such circumstances, to opt for silence by claiming descendancy from Beshimi stands as another kind of specious reasoning.

Another example of what I mean by small cultural facts can be seen in the "vulgar" manifestations of Shinto in Japanese life. Before a sumō match, the wrestlers toss salt in the ring in an elaborate ceremony. The act is a rite of purification for those who enter into battle. The same toss of salt occurs at funerals. Since man comes from the sea, we must be purified before we return to the sea. The purification is deliverance from the dirt of life as well as from the fear of death and defeat.

Also in the ceremony before a sumō match, each wrestler raises his leg and stomps on the ground, first on one foot and then on the other, a total of four times. A similar stomping on the ground is done by the kabuki actor, six times, when he strikes his theatrical pose on the portion of the stage that extends into the audience. In each case, the gesture is dramatic, and in each case, the stomping of the foot evokes an attempt by the performer to awaken the gods on the earth and to derive inspiration from them. Because devil gods also reside in the earth, the stomping of the foot, interestingly enough, is seen at the same time as an attempt to suppress evil spirits. Why one and not the other, though, is a question that has no answer. No doubt, from the Western point of view, the choice of evoking the good instead of the bad smacks of an opportunism, perhaps an irresponsible opportunism. Such opportunism, whatever the case, might be one of the characteristic features of the Japanese sensibility when more powerful external influences are encountered. Further, while such small cultural symbols await further interpretation and understanding, this cannot be expected to occur in the face of the foreign god Amatsukami.

Thus, the experiential methodology which I suggest here, which is based on Yanagita's methodology, is one of paradox: the science is unscientific. Yanagita believed that in sleep lie wisdom and truth, and his efforts were aimed at awakening and articulating this wisdom. This, of course, is the pursuit of literature and art. Literature and art can assume the ironies of truth, while scientific research, which seeks to define and confine it, will always remain outside. Even Yanagita, who observes with a keen eye, perhaps must also always remain outside of it. Observation may provide insight, but observation alone will not suffice for understanding.

Nonetheless, Yanagita's history of weeping stands as an exemplary piece of perceptive scholarship. Here, Yanagita suggested that a child wept because it was incapable of explaining its feelings logically. Without any reliance on stringent scientific research Yanagita demonstrated how placing oneself in the specific situation of a child could yield a profound understanding of the psychology of the child.

A third example of small cultural facts affording students of culture a glimpse of deeper truths can be seen in the story of the red torii in Japan. Torii, next to Mount Fuji, may be the most recognizable landmarks of Japan--they have even been known to appear next to each other on cushion covers and fans that are sold to tourists.

Torii seem also to have a Shinto history, and serve a different function than those on the Chinese continent, which were more common as simple gates. In Japan, they are referred to as the sacred gateway at the entrance to shrines. Two upright pillars support an upward curving lintel at the top of a straight cross-piece beneath. Sometimes torii stand off the shore in the sea. It is difficult to say precisely what the significance of torii is, however, or why it is so common a Japanese symbol.

Historically, torii have been closely related to death. They were constructed to stand at the front of the emperor's tomb and in this way served as a marker of reverence, not unlike a cross perhaps.

On the other hand, torii also act as a shield for the world of the living from the world of the dead. They suggest the distance that people should maintain from death and thus serve as a marker of danger and caution. This contradiction in attitude, while unmistakable, is not untoward. In fact, it is my belief that torii, symbolic in themselves, are a product of this contradiction.

My supposition is that torii exist as a framework, a physical as well as symbolic framework, through which the Japanese can embrace, for example, the disparate strains of aesthetic tradition and technological futurism, the more indigenous and the clearly foreign. Japan, an island country, is geopolitically and geographically related to the sea. Its cultural base is from the South Seas, its civil service system from China, and its technology from the West. There is, of course, a culture that is peculiar to the Japanese, but it is hardly self-generated. Imitation of a foreign influence was always the first step; then came innovation and transformation to make the influence suited to the Japanese.

Through the physical framework of the torii, a person on the shore views both sea and sky. The sense of what lies beyond is offered. Etymologically, this sense of beyond is the sense of ama, the same ama of Amatsukami, the foreign god. In ancient times, the word ama referred ambiguously to both sea and sky, representing what was unknown, whether death or curiosity or enchantment. Thus, torii came to suggest both an openness to and acknowledgment of the world beyond Japanese shores.

Such acknowledgment is manifested, I believe, in a nostalgia, a sentimentality, for a past, for the homeland. In this case, the homeland is the South Seas, and the manifestation is the Japanese garden, which recreates the image of ocean and shore and mountain. Etymologically, this suggestion is again borne out in that the word for garden has not always been niwa, as it is now; previously shima, which means island, meant garden. The Japanese garden thus stands as an abstraction of the utopian nature of the South Seas.

The earlier torii were constructed either of shiroki, stripped wood, or kuroki, unstripped wood. That torii were unpainted was not, I think, an aesthetic choice. Indeed, when Chinese culture was introduced into Japan and the Japanese became aware that temples on the Chinese continent were painted red or green, the Japanese were quick to adopt the fashion. Immediately, many of the torii in Japan were painted bright red. It did not matter that the significance of the red paint, which for the Chinese was symbolic of the blood of animals sacrificed to the gods, did not apply to the Japanese who did not make such sacrifices. The Japanese were so enamored with foreign things that imitation was immediate and certain.

The history of response to foreign influence is taken a step beyond imitation in the development of the Japanese linguistic form. Kanji, Chinese characters (ideographs) from the Han dynasty, constitute the Japanese written language. But using the Chinese characters as a base, Japanese women from the Heian court established the system of kanamoji. The word kana comes from karina, which means an assumed name, as opposed to mana, which means the real name. If mana is taken to represent kanji, Chinese characters used by men, then karina comes to represent kanamoji, the phonetic alphabet borrowed from kanji and used initially only by women, whose power in court was then in decline. Kanamoji was essentially a simplification of kanji, indicative of sound rather than concept.

In linguistic development, sound is more critical than form. The written form of Chinese characters may be more universal and more efficient in uniting an empire, but it is sound which preserves the more restricted local dialects and which, incidentally, is the basis of the first communication between mother and child. (In fact, kanamoji, now called hiragana, was initially known as the women's language.) Because of this emphasis on sound, the Chinese characters were innovated upon, as it were, to create a language that is specific to Japan: both the more universal Chinese characters as well as the more "particular" phonetic kanamoji are used.

Innovation and transformation as responses to foreign influences can also be seen in ceramics. When Chinese ceramics were first introduced into Japan, Japan was without doubt far behind in both production and technique. But the Japanese were quick to develop a refined sense of appreciation. Temmoku bowls (Sung 960-1280) brought back to Japan by Zen Buddhist priests who had studied near Tien Mu Shan (produced in Japanese as temmoku), were highly prized because the dark color of the glaze was perfectly suited to the bright green tea in the tea ceremony. The most valued of the temmoku was the yohen, which was accomplished by an accident of the kiln that sprinkled the black glaze with star-like bursts of color. The Japanese appreciation of this type of temmoku was not only for its beauty and suitability for tea ceremony, but also for the fact that chance had produced them.

With such appreciation for temmoku, the Japanese attempted their own ceramics, and the result was raku. Although raku's origins are clearly imitative, the technique is unique to Japan. Under the guidance of Rikyū, the founder of Japanese tea ceremony and a proponent of a Japanese cultural nationalism, Chōjirō developed raku, a peculiarly Japanese style of ceramics.

The next major period is Azuchi-Momoyama (1568-1600). It was a period when Japan's level of production was quite high and it was taking steps towards modernization. She was also in an aggressively expansionist mood--especially towards Korea, for example. Historians often label this period as a 'masculine' age. Although that is in many senses true I would like if possible not to forget completely the shadow world of women's culture.

Japan's expansionist ambitions of this era were to a certain extent made possible by its improved economy. The level of iron and rice production was high. Up until the fifteenth century the Japanese and Korean GNP's had been roughly the same, but suddenly Japan's production increased. The reason was that Japan had fuel. Iron production requires enormous amounts of fuel. China used both coal and wood, and forestry became big business. Japan's situation was peculiar unto itself. During the months of June and July the climate in Japan becomes tropical, like Thailand and Burma. The hot, wet conditions are perfect for tree growth, giving Japan almost limitless energy. But at the same time as being blessed with the profits of a tropical climate, Japan also has the four distinct seasons: spring, summer, autumn, winter, which are shared by most 'civilized' countries. The countries which have these seasons are quite few but have generally been responsible for most recent cultural history. It's often said that Japan 'suffers' from her climate. I disagree. If anything Japan has two extra seasons--the rainy season and the typhoon season--making the climate excellent for rice production, and for the provision of fuel.

The political centers of Japan, Kyoto and Tokyo, are well-known but it was during the Momoyama period that the industrial centers of Chūbu, based around Nagoya, and Chūgoku, based around Hiroshima, began to increase in importance. Of course, the improved iron and rice production was an important factor, but perhaps more so was the skill of Oda Nobunaga. He encouraged economic development by introducing a free market. And using the increased economic performance as a background, he advanced Japanese modernization considerably. It seems that he particularly disliked Buddhism and the traditional Kyoto aristocracy, and the power that they respectively held, and he was even willing to embrace Christianity in an attempt to destroy these traditions. Perhaps his most important invention, however, was a new way of war. He gave each soldier a gun and kept up a constant stream of fire by rotating ranks. With this method he overcame the dangerous waiting time which was necessary with matchlock-type weapons.

Toyotomi Hideyoshi inherited the legacy of Nobunaga and soon united Japan under his rule. Not content with mere rule, however, he set off on several escapades to Korea (1592-1598). The reason he went is often said to be a kind of political nationalism. He was apparently annoyed by the refusal of the Ming dynasty in China to acknowledge Japan as any more than a backward country. So, using money provided by Japan's improved economy he attempted to demonstrate Japan's worth. It's important to remember that Hideyoshi was a 'working class' politician. He was not an elevated member of the aristocracy or samurai classes. He was definitely a 'Hitler-type' politician.

Strangely for a soldier, Hideyoshi's ultimate ambition was to go flower-viewing. To this end he collected cherries from all over Japan and planted them all together in one area, essentially creating his own version of nature, which I will call 'third nature'. The word 'nature' is, I think, vague in its meaning. Botanically speaking, true nature is probably the primeval forest of 20,000 years ago which might be called 'first nature'. 'Second nature' can be seen, for example, in the scenery around Arashiyama. Here nature is essentially preserved but has been arranged, or artificialized, to human preferences. The mountain cherry, which is important to the Japanese, fits, I think, into this category. The Japanese love for this cherry is expressed in its role as an indicator of the rice harvest: if the petals fall quickly it will be a bad harvest, if not then it will be good. For this reason, at the Imamiya Shrine in Kyoto there is a festival to encourage the cherry blossoms to stay on the tree. In this way the cherry tree entered Japanese folklore. A much more dramatic demonstration of the beliefs of the Japanese people is 'Yoshino Senbonzakura'--a thousand cherry trees on Yoshino mountain. Each tree was planted by an individual as a sign of his faith in the superstition which connects the cherry tree with the rice harvest.

To return to Hideyoshi's 'third nature', it is completely artificial. There were no cherries at all in Daigo temple, but Hideyoshi brought trees from all over Japan and planted them so that they would flower, in turn, for a period of 4 or 5 days. I think this was the beginning of Japan's 'kitsch', popular culture. Japanese culture was then divided into two: the rather lonely 'shadow' culture and the much more energetic and prominent 'kitsch' culture of which Hideyoshi was probably the founder.

In the Momoyama period, Rikyū represents 'neglected' culture. It was the culture of _wabi_ and _sabi_, and represented the best of Japan's traditions, but was by nature 'particular'. In opposition to this, Hideyoshi, representing the lower-level, more universal culture, built the gaudy gold tearoom of Osaka castle. Hideyoshi and Rikyū represent the front and back cultures of the period, and both of them were guilty of forms of nationalism: Hideyoshi of blatant political nationalism and Rikyū of a form of cultural nationalism; that is, he rejected Chinese and Korean tea bowls in favor of those produced in Japan. The end of the relationship between Hideyoshi and Rikyū is significant: political power destroyed the cultural power: the 'front' culture overpowered the 'back' culture: that is, Hideyoshi ordered Rikyū's suicide.

The next period I want to look at, and which incidentally brings about 'fourth nature', is the Bunka/Bunsei period (roughly 1800-30), the culmination of Edo culture. During this period, at Asakusa in Tokyo, 'fourth nature' makes its appearance. Asakusa, dedicated to Kannon, was a popular place for the 'populace' to go and pray. As it was patronized almost exclusively by the lower classes it became very lively, almost festival like, and certainly more secular than religious. The atmosphere was always like that of the cherry-season, and so, as a result, a cherry tree which flowers for a long time was cultivated. Called 'Someiyoshino', it was a new type, made artificially using a Yoshino cherry as a base. It has a mass of flowers and they bloom for much longer than ordinary mountain cherries. This new cherry was then planted near Asakusa temple, and the lower classes adopted the previously exclusive habit of flower viewing. The whole area became a center of attraction. Hanging from the branches of the trees were _tanzaku_--strips of paper on which were written the names of local hostesses.

This is a perfect example of the relaxed attitude of the Japanese towards sex and drink and also of their almost unrestricted commercialism. Certainly, I think it's a practice which may be difficult for non-Japanese to understand.

This artificially grafted cherry is, as I've said, 'fourth nature'. In the Shōwa period (1926-), 'fifth nature' appears. With the introduction of the plastics industry, a completely artificial, plastic cherry was made. It was used as decoration to induce a party atmosphere in all places at all times of the year and was the culmination of the development of Japanese 'kitsch' culture. The five Japanese natures and the history of the cherry are very important as one example of the development of Japanese culture.

I introduced the Bunka-Bunsei era in connection with Japan's cherry culture. I'd like briefly to return and look more closely at the details of this apex of Edo-period culture (1600-1868). Its most striking characteristic was pervasive consumerism. Out of the one million population of Edo, about half were consumers--that is, non-productive members of the community. Neither artisans nor merchants, the samurai were essentially government employees. Although originally they could have been equated with European knights, they now played a different role. Their task was to manage the feudal organization, to encourage trade and production. In effect, they acted as equivalents of the present-day minister of trade.

The population of Edo topped one million at the beginning of the eighteenth century, more than a hundred years before London or Paris. The balance of the population of Edo was also important. As I've said, there was a high proportion of consumers (non-productive members of society). This is a very modern social trend and one in which Edo was far ahead of the major European capitals. Kyoto and Osaka were different; they still had a high proportion of artisans. A by-product of this booming economy was the first department store in the world, Mitsukoshi (at that time it was called Echigoya) in Ginza, which specialized in dry goods. It was also remarkable in its way of trading--it was the first store in the world to sell only at the marked price. It never offered reductions. The Mitsukoshi way of advertising was another first. When it rained, customers were lent umbrellas printed with the Mitsukoshi logo. They then walked the streets of Edo as free advertising. This method of course is used freely nowadays, on customer shopping bags.

I'd now like to look briefly at urban development in Japan. The first major city was Kyoto, followed by Osaka, then Tokyo. Founded in 794, Kyoto led Japan for nearly one thousand years. During this period Kyoto was not only the political center of Japan, but was also the center for wealth, founded mostly on the textile industry, which continues to this day. In the 1700's, however, Japan's economic expectations suddenly increased and it became necessary to concentrate industry in one place. A center was needed which could handle not only the textile industry but also the distribution of the increased rice production. The new center was Osaka, especially the area called Senba which is linked by the Yodo river to Kyoto. In this area huge and powerful wholesalers began to trade, basing their economy on the silver rather than the gold standard. Although these wholesalers had tremendous power, their way of trading was not very up-to-date. A more contemporary style of trading is to sell in smaller lots straight to the consumer, which explains why supermarkets now are more up-to-date than department stores. The relationship between Osaka and Tokyo reflects this difference. Osaka did develop as a center of wealth in Kansai, but its trading methods were out-of-date and so it, and the silver standard, both lost to the rising Edo economy. In the 1800s, Edo took over as the economic and political heart of Japan. Nagoya and Hiroshima, of course, continued to expand as industrial centers and now with the boom in the electronics industry, they have been joined by other areas. Places like Akita, Kōchi, Miyazaki have become centers of silicone chip production. They are new as industrial areas and so there has been little opposition to new development, and the workforce is cooperative. Air transport also makes communication with Tokyo easy.

To assume that all of Japan is in an equal state of prosperity would be a complete misinterpretation. There are places in decline and places which are booming. Osaka lost its power to Tokyo quite early--in the early 1800's. One of the main reasons was that Edo

developed the new way of retailing, and of course had a high proportion of 'consumers' in its population. Another reason, more in-
direct, was the improved standard of education, and especially the
literacy rate. In Tokyo, the ordinary people used this knowledge to
set themselves up in small businesses of their own. And it was
partly this economic energy which was responsible for the development
of the unique 'Edo' culture. Such art forms as Ukiyo-e and Kabuki
which were nurtured in Edo, are regarded as the best of Japanese
urban culture. Western scholars often claim that Japan's modern age
began with Meiji, and that the culture of Edo is the culture of an
outdated feudal society. I disagree entirely. I think that the
modern age began in this Bunka/Bunsei period and that the foundations
for present day Japan were laid in the culture of Edo.

* * * * * *

My effort in this paper has been both an apology for and a
demonstration of the methodology of Yanagita, who has influenced my
own work greatly. Yanagita's methods have been criticized, I know,
because of his essayistic, unsystematic, unscientific, arbitrary
style. He has also been criticized for his use of second-hand field
research. But I do not think these criticisms are entirely just.
Yanagita's strength is his insight, and this insight was born from a
situational understanding of custom and habit. His unsystematic
methodology derives from the fact that custom and habit are not systematic, and that the imposition of science cannot bring order where
none exists. It is the experience of custom and habit that is more
critical, therefore, than statistical analysis.

That Yanagita has made use of second-hand field research ought
not to warrant great attention. Meiji Taishōshi (A History of the
Meiji and Taishō Periods) was written almost entirely on the basis of
newspaper clippings. While current sociological methods would find
this unscholarly, Yanagita's insight seems not to have suffered. In

fact, I would contend that in the case of Yanagita, the weaker the documentation, the deeper the insight.

Together with Yanagita Kunio, one other person has had a strong influence on the development of my work, Kon Wajirō. Kon Wajirō was thirteen years younger than Yanagita Kunio and was originally his pupil. He broke away from the main stream of Yanagita's ethnology and began a new branch called in Japanese 'kōgengaku', which he translated into the composite word 'modernologio'--in English, modernology. Yanagita was infuriated at this upstart invention and immediately excommunicated Kon. They never reconciled. Kon was of course very much influenced by Yanagita's methods of ethnology, but claimed that his discipline was different. Kon's interest was in the exploration of the future based in the present, whereas Yanagita was concerned with the investigation of the past found in the present. Broadly speaking Yanagita Kunio was involved with rural ethnology and Kon Wajirō with urban ethnology. Both scholars achieved quite remarkable results, but Yanagita published more books and is far better known in both Japan and abroad. I think, however, that in the future, in the development of new academic disciplines, Kon Wajirō is likely to exert an influence equivalent to that of Yanagita Kunio.

Yanagita Kunio and Kon Wajirō share one major accomplishment-- they invented an originally Japanese discipline devoted to the scientific analysis of modern society. It is not easy to find a foreign equivalent. Yanagita's minzokugaku is probably closest to ethnology, but it was only recently with the appearance of micro-sociology that a Western subject similar to Kon's kōgengaku has been developed. Minzokugaku and kōgengaku can both be classed as kokugaku, although originally the word referred to the studies of such founders of the Meiji Restoration as Motoori Norinaga--that is, an investigation and interpretation of the roots of Japanese culture through a study of, for example, literature or the indigenous religion, Shinto. Post-Meiji Restoration, however, Yanagita and Kon's kokugaku were not involved with the religious origins of the Japanese as preserved in systems or institutions but were rather concerned with uncovering the essentially Japanese characteristics of society and culture using the methods of a Japanese academic discipline. And as a result, both of them were excluded from the Japanese academic world, which was generally absorbed in the pursuit or imitation of Western styles of academia. Most academics at the time worked by attaching comments to foreign texts, very different from the more direct methods chosen by Yanagita or Kon.

Their response to the limits of the academic world brought about a kind of 'counter-consciousness', a reaction which is, I think, characteristic of Japanese culture. Japan has always been a border country and has had to contend with the influence of a major outside culture to establish her own identity. In a sense, Motoori Norinaga's work was a reaction against the foreign influences in Japan, an attempt to find a different character. I think you could say that it was a kind of cultural nationalism. Although it can't be classified as an academic discipline, cha no yu, developed by Rikyū, was also an example of this cultural nationalism--this reaction which fueled the drive to create an identity. In Rikyū's assertion that, for example, Japanese tea bowls were not only equal to but possibly superior to those from China lay traces of this 'counter-consciousness', which can later be found in the work of Yanagita and Kon.

The factors which made up this counter-consciousness were not the same as those which contributed to the development of major civilizations. Rather it was made up of the small, the weak things of life, elements of what I call the Japanese sensibility. Instead of concentrating on, for example, major and well-thumbed works of literature, Yanagita and Kon turned to previously overlooked ways and customs, including lullabies, nursery rhymes, children's games, riddles and songs--in other words the ordinary, the fundamental things of life which comprise a culture.

Kon, who approaches his subject through architecture, was not interested in massive prestigious buildings, but rather in the tiny houses of the prostitutes of Shinjuku in Tokyo. He made a detailed record of the personal belongings in the cupboard of one of these prostitutes, a piece of research which is now invaluable and was until then unheard of. Half a century later, this record of the things in her possession provides a fascinating look into her beliefs and sentiments. It is also a good example of Yanagita's and Kon's approach, which used artifacts as indicators or records of social history.

Yanagita was concerned with the meaning of nursery rhymes, children's songs, games, etc., which of course have now become a popular subject of academic attention. These games and songs reveal the true nature of their own particular culture as well as having a strange, universal appeal. Yanagita was struck by the importance of these customs which had previously been ignored by such kokugaku scholars as Motoori. He recognized their valuable role in the continuation of culture, despite their apparent insignificance. In looking for the essence of Japanese culture in the higher forms of literature or organized religion, the scholars had overlooked the richest source of clues to Japanese characteristics. Common to both Yanagita and Kon is the paradox that what is apparently most insignificant is in fact most important. They were both working in the same field but were looking in opposite directions. Yanagita was concerned with examining the customs of the past from a position in the present, in other words, viewing permanence as a medium for comparison.

My own studies are concerned with modern society and the elements of the past which survive in it. In this respect, Yanagita's records are invaluable. Perhaps the most relevant and most modern of his books is Meiji Taishōshi, a history of the Meiji and Taishō eras. It was published in 1930 and was, I suspect, though this is only a personal suspicion, written as a reaction to Kon's breakaway in 1927 to form his own kōgengaku. I think Yanagita wrote it to demonstrate to Kon that it was possible to produce an analysis of modern society using the method of his ethnology. He was in fact taking a stand

similar to that Kon adopts in his books K̄ogengaku and Jukyōron. But
I don't today want to launch into a comparative analysis of Yanagita
and Kon. Instead, I want to choose just a few examples which illustrate the influence both scholars have had over my work.

In Meiji Taishōshi, for example, I was particularly interested
in the link Yanagita found between sake and the status of women. In
Japanese, the word for an important woman, or the mistress of the
house, is toji. The etymology of this word is the same as the word
toji (written with different characters), which refers to the person
who makes sake. It is clear from this that women were originally
responsible for the production of sake. Even now, in areas of New
Guinea, a drink is served which is made from rice first chewed by
women and then fermented. In Japan, the link between sake and the
kami is very close; that women were responsible for chewing the rice
and making the sake indicates their role as sacred servants/represen-
tatives. Even nowadays, in shrines sake is served by female miko.
From their position as representatives of the kami, women inherited
the privilege of making, managing, and distributing sake. It was
Yanagita who uncovered this link between women as managers of the
sacred sake and their elevated position in the home. He proposed
that for women to serve sake was far from a lowly and humble duty.
Rather it reflected their superior position as sacred messengers. In
Japan, drink was far less common than in the west and was usually re-
served for festivals; so when Japanese drank on these occasions they
believed that they were drinking together with the kami--and it was
women who acted as the intermediary. Even now the pleasure Japanese
men take in being served a drink by a woman is not purely sexual.
The woman represents the kami and provides the direct link with this
tradition. Without women it would not feel as if one were really
drinking sake.

That Japanese women were respected as toji--as managers of the
sake--shows that they had demonstrated their general ability to manage. I think the following is also one of Yanagita's explanations

--that it was Japanese womens' ability to manage which was responsible for the fact that the Chinese system of eunuchs managing the
Imperial household was not imported into Japan. Compared with China,
women of the Japanese aristocracy came from much humbler backgrounds,
tended to be more practical, and were proficient in the use of the
abacus. This made eunuchs superfluous as managers. Another, rather
more ironic, explanation is that, compared with the Chinese court,
the Japanese court was so small and insignificant that even women
could manage it! Whatever the reason, it is clear evidence of the
management skills of Japanese women. It may come as a surprise to
many non-Japanese to find that this tradition of women managing the
household continues today. Roughly 80 percent of Japanese men still
hand over their unopened pay packets to their wives, and in return
survive on a small monthly allowance.

How great were the social changes which took the activity of
drinking out of the control of the wives and transferred it to bars
and the control of geisha or hostesses! The familiar image of the
samurai, sake bottle in hand roaming through the streets of Edo seems
to be a fabrication, or at least it happened very rarely. In the
early Edo period there were very few bars; drinking was mostly done
at home under the watchful eye of the mistress of the house. Only
the very wealthy could afford the luxury of outside entertainment, of
ochaya in the pleasure quarters. With the flowering of the Edo
period, geisha and bars began to increase. Nevertheless, it wasn't
until the 3rd decade of Meiji (the 1890s) that the custom of eating
and drinking out really became popular and possible for most people.

This twilight world of downtown bars took entertainment out of
the home. In one sense, the work of a geisha is to serve sake to men
and is therefore considered a low-class job. But Japanese society
provides a convenient paradox which reversed their status. The
geisha was well-trained in the traditional arts and therefore de-
served respect as an artist. Thus her job achieves social respecta-
bility. The establishment of bars where men could drink outside was

responsible for a kind of social security system, which allowed di-
vorced or widowed women an alternative to falling onto disrepute. In
the many bars which crowd the downtown areas of modern Japan this
system continues. This entertainment world, which is on the fringes
of society, paradoxically guards some of the strongest traditions of
the mainstream of culture.

 With the spread of bars, the biggest change was that the management of _sake_ was taken from the hands of the wife and out of the home
territory. The man now did his drinking elsewhere and the wife remained at home guarding the household. Drink, the wife, and the home
became completely separated. And one reason was that the wife no
longer considered the serving of _sake_ a privilege, as a sign of
power, and instead saw it as a form of service. This was a major
change of values, and probably came about as a result of Western influence in the post-Meiji period. Guests and then husbands were
banished from the house, which the wife then fortified as the symbolic heart of the family, of the familial ego. The revitalization
of family life in Japan in the early 20th century was equivalent to
the movement in England in the 1930's, encouraged by Queen Victoria,
when the fireplace came to be regarded as the symbol of domestic
bliss. The equivalent symbol in Japan was I think the chabudai, the
low table, which became the focus of family life. This method of
seeing changes in social habits and customs through objects is a
method which I owe to Yanagita and Kon.

 The emergence of the family ego also brought changes in the
style of eating. It was usual in Japan for each member of the family
to have his own separate tray. But in the late 19th century, the
chabudai made its appearance. The family now abandoned their individual trays and gathered around the table to eat together. This
produced a kind of family spirit, a sense of unity. It is ironic
that just as the influence of European style individualism was being
felt in Japan, the Japanese gave up their individualistic style of
eating and instead formed a family group round the table. Evidence

of this social change can be found in Natsume Sōseki's novel <u>Mon</u>. The hero runs away with a friend's wife and together they try to start a life away from their relations and the rest of society in Tokyo. And as a symbol, as a focus of their attempt to form an identity, there is a <u>chabudai</u> table.

And so, in Japan, as the wife came to regard the home as her family territory, with the table as a symbol of its unity, so the husband was driven to meet his guests outside. The husband escaped downtown and was responsible for the development of the flourishing night life of most Japanese cities. After the war, however, yet another change took place in the pattern of the home life of the Japanese: the introduction of the dining kitchen and the replacement of the low table (<u>chabudai</u>) with the Western-style dining table. But the family structure had already begun to fall apart. The husband took every opportunity to drink out, the children retired to their rooms with instant food of their choice, and the wife was left alone. Wives who realized their plight were thus responsible for the introduction of the DK--dining kitchen--an attempt to restore the heart of the family and bring the group back together again. And the focus of this room was not the traditional <u>tokonoma</u>, or an ornament or flower arrangement, but an electrical gadget: the mixer/blender. The mixer was introduced into Japan after the war, when Japan was still so poor that most Japanese hardly had the ingredients to put in it. Everyone expected that it wouldn't sell, but it did. Japanese women saved the money and installed the blender as a centerpiece on the dining table. With this gadget as an incentive, the dismembered family reassembled round the table. The new gadget was modern, motorized, and enamelled; it reminded the Japanese of the magazine pictures of the luxuries of American home life, luxuries which they thought were unattainable. The appearance of this one machine contributed to a large degree to pulling the Japanese family back together again and enticing them back into the wife's territory.

This is how changes in Japanese social customs were reflected in the lives of ordinary Japanese. I would like now to look briefly at the divisions of the traditional Japanese living space; these divisions in the Japanese home are, I think, fundamental to an understanding of the Japanese sensibility. In this analysis I am again indebted to Yanagita Kunio and Kon Wajirō. They were responsible for first making a clear division of the Japanese house into three levels: doma (earth floor), itanoma (wooden floor), and tatami (the straw mats). The tokonoma, which held such an important position in Japanese aesthetic sensibility, could be thought of as a fourth level. The Japanese levels are not equivalent to Western upstairs and downstairs. Instead the divisions mark the territory of different gods. The levels are, of course, physically different--mud, wood, or tatami--but more important are the abstract, more subtle distinctions which are hidden in customs, for example, the changes in footwear.

Traditional Japanese sandals, geta were originally made for walking in rice paddies. When going barefoot one ran the risk of disease or injury, so large, wooden geta were the practical answer. These geta were then also worn in the lowest level of the house--the doma--the kitchen area. On the next level, the itanoma, or floor, the geta were removed and slippers were worn instead. Moving up to the next level, tatami, slippers are removed and only bare feet are acceptable. This tatami area is the most sacred. It seems paradoxical that in a civilized culture shoes, which are usually regarded as a sign of civilization, should be relegated to the lowest position. Bare feet, which are a leftover from a more primitive culture, are paradoxically given the highest status. The reason is, I think, a question of sensibility, a matter of touch or direct contact between man and ground. The tatami are, of course, made of natural fibers and for the Japanese the most important and enjoyable state is one of contact between bare feet (or stocking feet) and tatami. Shoes or slippers would break the contact, interrupt the tactile link between man and his surroundings which is such an essential part of Japanese sensibility. The traditional way of walking, which can still be seen in Noh drama or the tea ceremony, is to slide the feet along the ground. Indigenous Japanese dancing, too, does not include shamanistic leaps into the air. Instead the dancer lovingly caresses the ground with bare feet, careful not to break the vital contact with the earth. In Japan, going barefoot is a primitive custom which has been absorbed by civilized culture and is still part of daily life. It is an example of the paradoxical relationship between primitive and civilized which is so often found in Japanese culture.

In the hierarchy of Western values since the 19th century, originality has been prized most highly. Beneath that falls imitation or silence. But it is my belief that all three levels have their own validity, their own human reason. Originality may be active and desirable, it is true, but it may occur more by chance, less by merit. Furthermore, according to Rousseau, the most human emotions are derived from passive experience. In this formulation, the hierarchy of good and less good, superior and inferior is invalidated. The examples of the Japanese language and ceramics, both of which were imitations, first, before their transformation into a peculiar Japanese application, demonstrate this well. Also, in certain circumstances, silence may be most desirable. Certainly, it is the space of silence in Noh, the presence of white in traditional painting, and the suggestion of emptiness in aesthetics that touches the Japanese most deeply.

It is with my favorite paradox, that the most superficial is the most profound and the apparently most important is the most insignificant, that I would like to end this lecture. The inspiration, rather than the methodology, behind this approach certainly came from both Yanagita Kunio and Kon Wajirō. I have often used this paradox as a defense and an explanation of Japanese culture. I was once attacked by an Indian scholar who claimed that the Japanese were very superficial--that unlike say China or India there is no major philosophy or religion at the core of their culture. This is a criticism

I've heard many times from both Japanese and non-Japanese. The apparent religious inconsistency of the Japanese is often remarked upon. It is not uncommon, for example, for a Japanese to have a Shinto baptism, a Christian wedding and a Buddhist funeral. But this to me is not opportunism or atheism. It is a different attitude toward religion. Japanese religious sense is not contained in one doctrine, but rather is expressed in everyday life, in everyday sensibility. Buddhist, Shinto and Confucian doctrines are of course a part of Japanese culture, but I don't think they are the major form of expression of the Japanese religious spirit. Instead, this is shown in everyday life and artifacts. It appears, for example, in the influence of Zen Buddhism on food or architecture, or the traces of Shinto in ikebana. Japanese religion has become an aesthetic sense that is expressed in the customs, manners, and objects of everyday life. Religion lies on the periphery rather than in the core of society. Instead of a single doctrine which controls society from the center, Japanese society is controlled from the periphery. And it was Japanese society with its spiritual heart in the periphery of life rather than in a monotheistic core which produced the ethnology and modernology of Yanagita and Kon. These two academic disciplines were excluded from the mainstream of Japanese academia and were instead devoted to the exploration of the forgotten culture of Japan--to the small things of life.

Western scientific procedure depends primarily on deduction or induction. Because of this bias, the methodology of Yanagita, to Western scholars, seems unsound and unsystematic. Yanagita, as I understand his work, however, is concerned first with abduction. Once the phenomenon is apprehended or experienced--that is, after the abduction--the deduction or induction can follow. Yanagita's work is an example of the proper abduction.

AN APPROACH TO YANAGITA KUNIO'S VIEW OF LANGUAGE

Ōiwa Keibō

Yanagita's essay, "Teikyū shidan" (On the History of Wailing), reminds me of my own early experiences, as if somehow to verify his contention that people in the modern age have become less and less liable to cry.[1] I remember the vehement political arguments that I sometimes had with my father many years ago. As a highschool student I was highly agitated and politicized by the student movement of that era, and was interested, for some reason, in bringing my newly-learned political theories into the family circle. To my mother's surprise, an argument between my father and me over, for example, whether historical justice resided with Stalin or Trotsky, often became so emotional that it ended in a physical fight and brought me to tears. Yet I was decidedly not the "crybaby" type, and in fact never showed tears in my arguing and fighting outside the family circle.

It appears to me that two different levels of experience, or two different "discourses," were undifferentiated and intermingled in my arguments with my father. One level must have been based on political, ideological language. What, then, was the foundation of the other?

A possible answer seems to be offered by Yanagita, who suggests that there is an extra-linguistic sphere of expression in which one cannot but cry. In the essay mentioned above, he points out that the modern age places too much confidence in language:

> Today, a belief in the omnipotence of language seems
> all too prevalent. "But didn't you say so?," some-

---

1. Yanagita Kunio, "Teikyū shidan," in Teihon Yanagita Kunio shū, Vol. 7 (Tokyo: Chikuma Shobō, 1972), p. 327.

one might say, cross-examining you when you have in
fact said so but without actually believing it.
"What's so funny?" You are required to explain in
language even though you feel that you can only remain smiling. . . .

Also in the case of weeping, people often say, "What
do you mean by weeping?" or "Stop crying and tell me
the reason," but it is not so easy to comply with
the demand and to replace tears, right away, with a
verbal expression. . . .

It is because you find it impossible to express the
interior of your mind with words that you adopt the
method of wailing.[2]

It should be added that when Yanagita speaks of the waning reliance
on non-verbal expression in giving vent to one's interior states, he
includes in his horizon the diminishing importance of wailing and
laughing in ritual practice. As shown in the examples of the once-
widespread practice of nakimatsuri (lamentation ritual), for example,
and nakionna (a professional female mourner who is hired to weep at a
funeral), wailing used to play an important role not only as a spontaneous, individual phenomenon but also as a ritual.[3]

According to Yanagita, contemporary intellectuals are responsible for neglecting this significant realm of self-expression and
for believing that it is reducible to and able to be replaced by
language. They are, he argues, responsible for today's predominant
mental climate of "language worship."[4] It seems to me that his critical attitude toward language is, after all, a central axis around
which Yanagita's method of folklore study and his criticism of the
Japanese modern society revolves. In the following discussion I
should like to present an approach to this important problem.

Many of Yanagita's essays are characterized by the quite per-
sistent use of a set of methodological devices, which include

2. Ibid., pp. 330-331.

3. Ibid., pp. 332-333.

4. Ibid., pp. 329-330.

dialectology, etymology and conceptual dichotomy. By dialectology I do not mean the systematic study of dialects within the discipline of linguistics; rather, I am referring simply to Yanagita's lifelong endeavor to collect and document the diminishing vocabulary of regional languages throughout Japan. He often relied effectively on his knowledge of the lexical aspect of dialects in his attempt to interpret the activities of common people. In the belief that the documentation of dialect vocabularies constituted an indispensable part of the discipline of folklore studies, he wrote a great number of articles on the subject and also produced a series of folklore dictionaries.[5]

The second characteristic of Yanagita's method is his frequent recourse to etymology. The search for the root of a word often became so important as to constitute the central core of an argument in Yanagita's essays. This is one of the points at which scholars find Yanagita deeply immersed in the tradition of Kokugaku (Nativism). In his exegetical study of the Japanese classics and methodologies, the prominent nativist Motoori Norinaga (1730-1801) passionately searched for the archaic, and thus "ideal," form of Japan's native language. Motoori and others attempted to rediscover the "roots" of the present vocabulary, and to draw a strict distinction between words of foreign (Chinese) origin and those that were indigenous to Japan. They sought to distill a "pure," native language from the "mudwater" of contemporary culture.

The rediscovery of this pure language was believed to entail the restoration of magokoro, or the purest form of the Japanese native mentality: the "Yamato damashii."

In any case, Motoori's dichotomy between the native language and mentality, on the one hand, and the Chinese language and mentality on the other, seems to be akin to Yanagita's use of dichotomy, as mentioned above. It is reported by Tsurumi Kazuko that Yanagita once

---

5. Contained in <u>Teihon Yanagita Kunio shū</u>, Vol. 18 (Tokyo: Chikuma Shobō, 1972).

said, in a dialogue with Marion J. Levy, of Princeton University, that there are two kinds of people in Japan: those who speak round language and those who speak square language, and if he really wished to understand Japan, he would have to associate with the round-language speakers.[6] What he seems to have meant is the distinction between oral language and written language. For present purposes, I should like to pay particular attention to Yanagita's strategy of formulating a sharp contrast between pairs of words or concepts. A number of good examples can be found in his work Nihon no matsuri (The Festivals of Japan), where the whole discussion revolves around a series of what I shall call conceptual dichotomies.

It appears to me that a close examination of some cases in which these three methodological devices intermingle will bring us to a better understanding of Yanagita's view of language. For convenience, I should like to categorize some examples of the use of the device of conceptual dichotomy into three types: first, terms of native origin versus those of foreign (Chinese) origin; second, one native term versus another native term; and third, a dichotomy found within a term. (Note that with respect to debatable distinctions between native and non-native, I am merely following Yanagita's terminology.)

The contrast between matsuri and sairei will exemplify the first type. Let me summarize Yanagita's argument as it appears in Nihon no matsuri (see translation in Part III of this volume). In the course of Japan's modernization, people have become less and less aware of the difference between matsuri and sairei, both of which can be translated as "festival." This terminological distinction seems to reflect a substantial change that occurred in the ritual activities of common people. The change, which has both mental and be-havioral dimensions, could be characterized as the gradual subordination of matsuri to sairei. Sairei, a term of Chinese origin,

---

6. Tsurumi Kazuko, Hyōhaku to teijū to (Tokyo: Chikuma Shobō, 1977), p. 9.

represents a later transformation that has developed out of the ritual of the native form: matsuri. Therefore, in order to rediscover the constitution of this native form, it is necessary to distinguish matsuri elements from sairei elements. Despite the apparent dominance of urban festivals, there still remain in rural villages, as Japanese folklore studies have made clear, a small, inconspicuous, and traditional form of ritual which has not been greatly influenced by sairei elements. From the observable facts, then, we can roughly draw the boundary between matsuri and sairei. To the former belong such characteristics as small size, familial or communal participation, a rural setting, lack of florid or spectacular appearances, an emphasis on nighttime ritual, and the absence of both spectators and professionals. The latter may be characterized in terms of its large size, inter-communal participation, an urban setting, florid and spectacular scenes, daytime ritual, and the presence of spectators and ritual professionals.

Finally, Yanagita believes that the authenticity of matsuri as compared to sairei is supported by etymological characteristics of the ritual vocabulary, as demonstrated both historically, that is, on the basis of historical evidence, and spatially, with reference to dialectological evidence. The Festivals of Japan and About Our Ancestors contain quite a few instances of this sort but, for our present purposes, one example will suffice. Yanagita's implication is that the term matsuri is a nominalization of the action verb matsurou. Matsurou is not used in contemporary, standard Japanese, but it is known from historical and dialectological evidence that its meaning was "to be with (somebody superior)," and also "to serve (somebody superior)," "to offer to (somebody superior)," and so on. Yanagita seems to believe that the action of "being with" god (that is, in Yanagita's analysis, the ancestors), as that action continues to be implied by the root concept in the derivative word matsuri, signifies the essence of both the conduct and the idea of matsuri. From this point of view, sairei is regarded as a degenerate version of matsuri. Matsuri in its ideal form could imply such an intimate union between subject and object (god) as "being together," "staying together indoors," "eating together," and "talking to each other." Sairei, on the other hand, breaks up this intimacy by bringing mat- suri into the light of day, exposing it to spectators, and intro- ducing the professional priest as a mediator. Thus, if these sairei elements are really becoming more prevalent, as Yanagita seems to think, it would mean that there has been an alienation from matsuri.

The second of the three types of dichotomy can be most effec- tively seen in the contrast between mai and odori, both of which can be translated only as "dance." The Japanese dictionary tells us that mau, the infinitive form of mai, signifies the actions of "to go round and round," or "to spin round and round," whereas odoru, the infinitive form of odori, signifies the action "to jump." Yanagita explains:

> To put it simply, odori is an action, whereas mai is
> a chant or a speech followed by action as a by-
> product. . . . While earnestly and repeatedly speak-
> ing toward god, one goes off into ecstasies: the
> borderline state between man and god. This [transi-
> tion] is the original form of mai, and it is only in
> a gradual, later development that the pattern of
> movements has become pre-arranged.[7]

What is presented here is, first, the genesis of an action. To make this clearer, Yanagita cites a case of a similar kind. Nō theater, Japan's highly refined classical art form, has emphasized monogurui (being mad) as one of the most advanced techniques of mai. To be mad, in this sense, probably means a kind of subtle and spontaneous action that breaks through the mesh of scrupulously arranged move- ments.

Yanagita does not support this rather audacious conjecture about the term mai with any further reasonings, nor with material evidence. His conjecture is, however, quite informative in that it tells us of the linguistic view on which Yanagita's folklore studies

----

7. Yanagita Kunio, Nihon no matsuri, in Teihon Yanagita Kunio shū, Vol. 10 (Tokyo: Chikuma Shobo, 1969), p. 254.

127

are based. It seems that what Yanagita wants to show in his contrast of _mai_ with _odori_ has to do with two different aspects of language. In the case of _mai_, the action is conceived not from the outside but from within, in its process, or genesis. If Yanagita's "theory" is correct, in principle, we are not able to formulate such a phrase as _mai o mau_. When thus objectified, _mai_ is bereft of its basic root concept. On the other hand, one can, without going against the principle, make the phrase _odori o odoru_, since _odori_ contains, as its root concept an already objectified action.

The distinction between _hanashi_ and _katari_ is of a similar character. In his essay, "Sekenbanashi no kenkyū" (A Study of Chatting), Yanagita defines _katari_ in terms of a lecture, speech, or statement, which carries a certain formality, along with conventional phrasing and wording. Basically, it follows a written text. _Hanashi_ should be understood rather as idle talk, chit-chat, side-tracking, or everyday conversation within the familial or communal circle. This contrast, too, might be seen as pitting objectified language against the unobjectified. I recall a comment from one of Tsurumi Shunsuke's lectures at McGill University. According to Tsurumi, the _manzai_ (Japanese traditional, comic dialogue usually performed by a pair of dialogists) was originally a satirical representation of a dialogue between a central god and a local god.[8] The former, with his power of logical reasoning and speech, makes fun of the latter, who lacks even the ability to speak the sophisticated, central language. The _beshimi_, one of the masks used in Japanese traditional theater, according to Tsurumi, is probably an embodiment of the inner feeling of the local god. Its distorted face, with a wry mouth that expresses the local god's humiliation and his final recourse to silence is, however, so exaggerated as to make the audience smile. Yanagita, as if in support of the local god, also complains about the modern tendency to neglect the realm of _hanashi_.

___
8. Tsurumi Shunsuke, lectures at McGill University, 1980 (unpublished).

In the third type, Yanagita has detected a conceptual dichotomy within a word. For instance, he argues in "Teikyū shidan" that the verb naku has experienced over a period of time, an important change in its signification. Since the Chinese concept of "to wail," with its ideograph, prevailed in Japanese society, the word naku has become detached from its root concept, "to make a noise, or voice," and restricted to mean "to shed tears, to cry or weep with lament." The homonym naku, with its different ideograph, is used when birds and animals are led "to sing, coo, crow, bark, meow, moo, and so on," and a related verb, naru, when a thing proceeds "to sound." Yanagita believed that these words are also "drifts" from the same root. If Yanagita is right, we might be able to postulate a "conflict" within the word naku between the original root concept and the derivative one. Yanagita's contention seems to be that the gradual change from the former to the latter has exercised a great influence upon Japanese behavior.[9]

A similar change has taken place within the adjective kanashi, which originally signified various types of keen impressions and emotions, but, in modern standard Japanese, with its Chinese ideograph, signifies sadness. In some dialects, however, as Yanagita notes, there are still un-centralized usages of kanashi to mean "cute," "embarrassing," or "benumbed with cold."[10] Thus the dichotomy is, as it were, both temporal (the original versus the derivative) and spatial (central versus the local).

Where do the above examples lead us? In "Kagyū-kō" (Reflections on Snails), a remarkable study of hundreds of dialect words for "snail," Yanagita attempts to describe the way in which the creative power of "children or men's childishness, rather than the scholars

---

9. See Teihon Yanagita Kunio shū, Vol. 7, pp. 338-39.

10. Ibid., p. 337.

with their solemn looks, have determined language."[11] It seems to me that Yanagita persistently insists that there are two different kinds of language: language in daily life and language in scholarship. (Also note in this context that children and insanity play important roles in Yanagita's works.) In this regard, the following passage from About Our Ancestors might be helpful:

> The word dentō (tradition) is used at present to express the invisible legacy, but it gives one the feeling that there is only a passive way of thinking about it. Here we treat it as something more than that, something learned, actually practiced, and transmitted, worked with and shown, taught and made to be memorized, something that is handed down to the next generation from what can be ascertained by the ear and eye or something outwardly manifest.[12]

I think this passage also concerns two levels of language. One is a level at which a thing, an event or a life is observed and explained objectively, and the other is a level at which the objective, observational and explanatory attitude toward life has not yet emerged as such from the totality of life experience.

It is unlikely that Yanagita ever conceived of a purely subjective language and a purely objective language which could exist separately from each other in an actual, linguistic community. It seems to me, however, that he is eager to cast light on a dimension of language that represents the unobjectified moment of life. Let us recall his passion for tracing a word, historically (etymologically) and spatially (dialectologically), back to its root concept. That root concept, often a verb, is supposed to represent, so to speak, an archetype of human action. Yanagita seems to assume that the task of revealing the unobjectified aspect of language, and thus the search

---

11. Yanagita Kunio, "Kagyū-kō," in Teihon Yanagita Kunio shū, Vol. 18, p. 60.

12. Fanny Hagin Meyer and Ishiwara Yasuyo, tr., About Our Ancestors--The Japanese Family System, by Yanagita Kunio (Tokyo: Japan Society for the Promotion of Science and Ministry of Education, 1970), p. 40.

for the essential continuity between language and practice, constitute an indispensable part of his scholarship. It is in this sense
that Yanagita's minzokugaku (study of folkways) is believed to offer
a pointed criticism of society's general inclination toward what he
has called "language worship" and what Western social theory has
called "objectification."

FOLKLORE STUDIES AND THE CONSERVATIVE ANTI-ESTABLISHMENT IN MODERN JAPAN*

J. Victor Koschmann

Major post-World War II appreciations of the work of folklorist Yanagita Kunio have depicted him as a conservative who sought to preserve the ways of the past in the face of rapid change, and as a resister against the prewar establishment which centered on the state. I will attempt in this paper to assess and reconcile those claims in order better to understand the significance of Yanagita's discipline of Minzokugaku (Folklore Studies) in the context of modern Japanese history.

Bureaucratic "Renovationism"

The claims that Yanagita was both conservative and anti-establishment might on the face of it seem contradictory. Therefore, it is necessary to begin by constructing an image of the sort of "establishment" Yanagita might have confronted from the early-twentieth century onward. Bernard Silberman has argued that when faced with a crisis of legitimacy following their overthrow of the Tokugawa baku-fu, the Meiji leaders had been forced to establish a new rationale for state power. Part of their solution was a system for the allocation of social values which appealed, not primarily to an ideal of subjective choice on the part of a citizenry (e.g., elections plus full parliamentary responsibility), but rather to a utilitarian principle of objective rationality. This principle dictated that impartial experts ought to be able to make rational decisions to secure the greatest net benefit for the society treated as a whole

*I am indebted to Ms. Marilyn Ivy who read an earlier draft of this essay and made several very useful suggestions.

rather than as an aggregate of equal parts.[1] In order to perpetuate such a system, expertise and an ethos of impartiality had to be inculcated in an elite and guaranteed by a hierarchical network of schools which culminated, for the brightest and best, in one of the distinguished departments of the Imperial University. From there, most would be whisked off into public service.

Yet in its role as a guarantee of elite bureaucratic judgment, and therefore of government legitimacy, this system required at least an implicit consensus as to what sort of knowledge would provide the basis for expertise; that is, it was necessary to rely on a common definition of truth. If the knowledge imparted to the elite in school were not widely accepted as authoritative, then the elite's own capabilities would be cast into doubt and their decisions would not command respect. Thus, the very existence of the state depended upon an ability to produce and reproduce a body of truth. Here the most provocative formulation is provided by Michel Foucault:

> Truth is a thing of this world: it is produced only by virtue of multiple forms of constraint. . . . Each society has its regime of truth, its "general politics" of truth: that is, the types of discourse which it accepts and makes function as true; the mechanisms and instances which enable one to distinguish true and false statements, the means by which each is sanctioned; the techniques and procedures accorded value in the acquisition of truth; the status of those who are charged with saying what counts as true.[2]

In Foucault's view, this "general politics" exists more or less independently of the state. The needs it answers are primarily epistemological rather than political in the narrow sense, and its guard-

------

1. Bernard Silberman, "The Bureaucratic State in Japan: The Problem of Authority and Legitimacy," in Tetsuo Najita and J. Victor Koschmann, eds., Conflict in Modern Japanese History: The Neglected Tradition (Princeton, NJ: Princeton University Press, 1982), pp. 226-257.

2. Michel Foucault, Power/Knowledge: Selected Interviews & Other Writings, 1972-1977, ed. Colin Gordon (New York: Pantheon Books, 1980), p. 131.

ians include scientists, priests, novelists, and teachers as well as
government officials. Nevertheless, the social regime of truth generates a micropolitics of knowledge which in turn enters into relations of dependency with the sovereign powers that are exercised by
the state. Foucault's insights have a certain ready plausibility in
the Japanese case, because they seem capable of providing a useful
reconceptualization of the historical apparatus that modern Japanese
scholars have called the "emperor system."[3]

Foucault's imagery is suggestive, but no thorough attempt has
been made to apply his concepts to the prewar "emperor system," and
this essay will contribute very little in that regard. Perhaps it is
possible nonetheless to sketch out enough elements of the prewar
"regime of truth" to make possible a consideration of the anti-establishment potential of Yanagita's conservatism. First, the defeat
of natural rights as both an idea and a movement in the early part of
the Meiji period had left few alternatives to a belief in history as
an all-inclusive stream. Moreover, development in the midst of that
stream was believed by many to follow a basically unilinear track.
As Kenneth Pyle has observed, "Among bureaucrats and intellectuals
there was a strong belief in an inevitable path of universal historical development which all industrializing nations must follow."

---

3. On the "emperor system" see, for example, Tsurumi Kazuko,
Social Change and the Individual: Japan Before and After Defeat in
World War II (Princeton, NJ: Princeton University Press, 1970), pp.
89-114, and Masao Maruyama, Thought and Behavior in Modern Japanese
Politics (London: Oxford University Press, 1963), pp. 1-24. In
Japanese, Inoue Kiyoshi, Tennō-sei (Tokyo: Tokyo Daigaku Shuppankai,
1953), and Fujita Shōzō, Tenno-sei kokka no shihaigenri (Tokyo: Mir-
aisha, 1966). The case for an apparatus which functioned to maintain
a "regime of truth" in prewar Japan would have to be based on a number of works too numerous to list here. In addition to works by
Kenneth Pyle mentioned below, essays by Byron K. Marshall, James R.
Bartholomew and Peter Duus in Najita and Koschmann, Conflict, suggest
some directions, and include references to other relevant works. For
the negative, prohibitive side of such a regime one would do well to
rely on Richard H. Mitchell, Censorship in Imperial Japan (Princeton,
NJ: Princeton University Press, 1983).

134

Moreover, many believed that "technological changes would have the
same social consequences in every society and the pattern of social
development discernible in Western countries would likewise appear in
Japan."[4]

Confidence in the inexorable movement of history might in some
cases encourage government leaders to rely passively on natural processes but in twentieth-century Japan the opposite seems to have been
the case. Pyle goes on:

> Yet there was ambivalence; these were not necessarily
> ironclad laws of history. . . . The perceptive states-
> man understood the nature and direction of history,
> foresaw the outcome of change, adapted to it, and so
> paradoxically was even able to direct and control
> historical change. . . . That is, by acting early,
> before conditions worsened, it would be possible
> through state intervention to devise preventive poli-
> cies that would avert the extremes of social con-
> flict that had occurred in the West.[5]

The government bureaucracy, in other words, was not passive and
conservative but activist, or as some historians have suggested,
"renovationist" (kakushin). Particularly after the introduction to
Japan of ideas developed by the Young Historical School in Germany,
and the rapid ascendancy among elite bureaucrats of the tenets of
"social policy," the Japanese governing elite became increasingly
interventionist in its drive to prevent the social problems that had
plagued the early developers in Europe.

The parallel operation of an academic-bureaucratic apparatus
for the production and guarantee of a "regime of truth" is clearly
evident in the career of Kanai Noboru. He taught meliorative state
intervention to future bureaucratic and academic leaders at Tokyo
Imperial University for thirty-five years, 1890-1925, and was an

---

4. Kenneth B. Pyle, "The Technology of Japanese Nationalism:
The Local Improvement Movement, 1900-1918," Journal of Asian Studies
33 (1973), p. 53.

5. Ibid., p. 54.

administrator of the higher civil service examination for twenty-one
years. Kanai, his students, and others who supported a social-policy
approach to government eventually produced the Local Improvement
Movement (chihō kairyō undō) of the early twentieth century, the
Factory Act, the Conciliation Society for labor-management harmony,
the rural Cooperative Law, the Health Insurance Law, the Tenancy
Conciliation Law, and so on. In short,

> The generation of bureaucratic leaders in office
> during the interwar years had firmly rooted in their
> thinking the social policy ideal of a monarch and a
> neutral bureaucracy standing above narrow class in-
> terests, regulating economic conditions, reconciling
> opposing social forces, seeking to advance the in-
> terests of the whole by intervening in the economy
> to protect and integrate the lower classes into the
> nation.[6]

Takabatake Michitoshi has argued that as the new, kakushin
elite rose through the school system it was encouraged to throw off
the communal mentality of village society and to set itself against
everything "feudal, emotional, and conservative."[7] As a term used to
describe the forward-looking application of bureaucratic rationality,
therefore, kakushin also came to imply such qualities as nationalism,
faith in central planning, commitment to rising productivity, and
opposition to "feudal" social relationships. Kakushin officials
sought to coopt the left, and were critical of the hanbatsu cliques
based on regional loyalties, the ascriptive nobility, and also the
big bourgeoisie, whose expansive enterprises and financial combines
sought to distort national plans to accommodate their own "private,
selfish interests."[8] They upheld all that was "public," in the sense

---

6. Kenneth B. Pyle, "Advantages of Followership: German
Economics and Japanese Bureaucrats, 1890-1925," Journal of Japanese
Studies 1 (Autumn 1974), p. 162.

7. Takabatake Michitoshi, Tōron: Sengo Nihon no seiji shisō
(Tokyo: San'ichi Shobō, 1977), p. 202.

8. Ibid., p. 201.

of bureaucratically impartial and technically rational. Hence, "progressivism" in this sense is typified by the so-called kakushin kanryō ("progressive bureaucrats") of the mid-to-late thirties.

Takabatake further argues that this brand of progressivism was assimilated by the left in the form of the productivity theory (seisansei riron) that was developed by some intellectuals in the Marxist mainstream (Kōza-ha) and the prewar social-democratic parties. Then, following World War II, the socialist and communist parties tacitly inherited many aspects of this kakushin ideology without subjecting it to searching scrutiny.

Throughout Japan's modern era, therefore, the state sought through expansive forms of bureaucracy and cooptation to increase its own power and reinforce its authority. In order to do so, it was forced, because of its reliance for fundamental legitimacy on an intellectual and pedagogical "regime," to exercise sufficient hegemony over the production of knowledge to preserve the sanctity of its own definition of truth. Moreover, because of its acceptance of historical change and its "progressive" attempts to rationalize and develop society in accordance with historical trends, it placed "history" at the center of its "politics of truth" and took a direct interest in how history was represented.[9]

In sum, so long as progressivism is understood in terms of kakushin, it is apparent that in twentieth-century Japanese history

9. The Meiji emperor reportedly instructed that the basis for an orthodox history should be compiled under the auspices of the state. The result was the establishment of the Kokushi Hensan Kyoku (Bureau for Compilation of a National History), which changed its name several times but remained under direct political control until 1895. At that time, it was removed to the Literature Department of the Imperial University, where it was called the Shiryō Hensanjo (Center for Compilation of Historical Materials). Among its products were the Dai Nihon shiryō (Historical Documents of Great Japan) and Dai Nihon kumonjo (Classical Documents of Great Japan). See Tōyama Shigeki, Meiji ishin to gendai (Tokyo: Iwanami Shinsho, 1968), pp. 11-19.

conservative and anti-establishment need not be considered antonymic. There is, therefore, no reason prima facie why such a composite label should not be applied to Yanagita Kunio.

Yanagita as Kakushin Bureaucrat

No account of Yanagita's work in relation to the state and the surrounding establishment can afford to ignore Yanagita's own background as an elite product of the educational system, a graduate of Tokyo Imperial University, and bureaucrat in the Ministry of Agriculture and Commerce and other offices. He did not leave the government until he was forty-five years of age, and it appears that at least in the early stages of his career his views were decidedly kakushin in tendency. He had a strong consciousness of the "public," impartial role of the state. He believed that government leaders had to make policy in a manner that transcended all "private interests" and partial concerns, particularly those based on social class, in order to promote the historical progress ("shinpo hattatsu") of the country as a whole. With imagery reminiscent of Edmund Burke, Yanagita argued in 1906 that state policy should not respond mechanically to the current views of the majority of its citizens, but should take a longer range, more future-oriented approach:

> A nation's economic policy transcends and is independent of struggles based on the private interests of classes and must be decided on some other basis. The purposes of the state itself should never merely reflect the collective desires of the majority of its people or of a particularly powerful class. In other words, the sum of private interests does not constitute the public interest. To take an extreme case, even if the people of the nation in a particular era were unanimous in desiring a particular thing, the securing of that thing should not necessarily be adopted as national policy. That is because the people (jinmin), whom the state represents and whose interests it must defend, are not limited to those now living. The state also includes their countrymen who will be born in later generations, so there might be times when the interests of contemporaries will have to be sacrificed for the good of

the country's future residents. Of course, national
goals and the national interest cannot exist apart
from the people (kokumin), but the interests of the
whole country have an entirely different basis from
that of any particular part or class.[10]

Here, Yanagita's views are quite consistent with the Meiji
state's rejection of subjective, popular choice as the basis for
policy-making, and its reliance on the "impartial," objective rationality of a governing elite. This would tend to suggest that at least
early in his adult life, in the context of his official duties and
concerns, Yanagita was appropriately socialized as a kakushin bureaucrat.[11]

Kamishima Jirō believes that Yanagita retained an overly optimistic attitude toward the state, and suggests that this attitude was
eventually responsible for his failure to oppose World War II more
vigorously. In one of his postwar essays, Yanagita had expressed
regrets regarding his behavior during the militarist era:

> There were those who realized that things could not
> go on as they were. . . . But they were slow in
> starting to arrange a way [to do something about
> it]. They always gave first thought to such trivial
> considerations as the undesirability of being un-
> reasonable or of touching off a major debate, and
> because they proceeded in all too leisurely a manner
> they were too late, as events rapidly reached a dis-
> astrous state. If anyone is to be blamed it should
> not be the stubborn, old-fashioned ones, but rather
> those who had intentions but were too timid to put
> them in action, or who were too slow in realizing
> their goals. . . . I should confess that I myself am
> among them. But it does no good to repent now.

---

10. Quoted by Kamishima Jirō, "Minzokugaku to nashonarizumu,"
in Kamishima, Jōmin no seijigaku (Tokyo: Dentō to Gendaisha, 1972),
p. 154.

11. For a view of Yanagita's early bureaucratic career that
emphasizes his encouragement of local autonomy and early criticism of
the government, see Tsurumi Kazuko, Hyōhaku to teijū to (Tokyo:
Chikuma Shobō, 1977), pp. 200-202.

Rather, I must immediately begin work to make
amends.[13]

It would, therefore, be prudent to suppose that throughout his
career Yanagita was basically receptive to state authority and probably never intentionally set himself or his work against the state
itself in any fundamental way. Such an attitude would be consistent
with Yanagita's belief that scholarship should be useful in improving
the lives of the common Japanese people, if we assume that in the
final analysis he hoped the state would provide an agency for that
improvement.

Nevertheless, such an assumption does not preclude the possibility that aspects of his scholarship, and the discipline of Folklore Studies he founded, often worked at cross purposes to the ideology on which the state depended, and thus in retrospect--regardless
of Yanagita's own intentions--he might be shown to have effected a
mode of resistance against the prewar establishment.

Yanagita and the Conservative "Counter-Utopia"

Hashikawa Bunsō has argued that if Yanagita's world view is
assessed from the perspective of his discipline of Folklore Studies,
one finds it to be consistent with an original, or "pure," conservatism. While this conservatism shares certain tendencies with the
kakushin ideology, it also differs from it in fundamental respects.
Common elements include the conviction that the human world is in
constant flux. Yanagita often made statements to the effect that
"There has never been a life situation [yo no naka] that did not
change; old and new have always been in constant confrontation.
. . ."[13] Yanagita also shared with the kakushin ideology an opposi-

---

12. Quoted in Kamishima, Jōmin no seijigaku, p. 152.

13. Quoted in Hashikawa Bunsō, "Hoshushugi to tenkō: Yanagita
Kunio to Shiratori Yoshichiyo," in Shisō no Kagaku Kenkyūkai, ed.,
Kyōdō kenkyū: tenkō, Vol. II (revised edition) (Tokyo: Shisō no
Kagaku Kenkyukai, 1978), p. 230; quoting from Yanagita, "Tōseifū to
mukashifū."

tion to the bourgeois universalist perspective of the Enlightenment,
which they branded as unhistorical and abstract. These similarities
are of great importance to any attempt to assess the political implications of Yanagita's work.

The differences, however, are also significant. Using concepts
and distinctions drawn from the work of Karl Mannheim, Hashikawa
compares Yanagita to such "original" conservatives as Justus Möser:
so called because they resisted the decline of conservatism into a
self-infatuated romanticism, and remained apart from those ideologues
who made the conservative orientation into a comprehensive "theory"
in order to resist liberalism. Yanagita shared with Möser a "conservative reformism" that always attached itself closely to concrete
particulars. Hashikawa quotes Yanagita:

> [Required is a] form of scholarship that is based on
> actuality, an attitude that does not despise the
> most common reality, a research method which, when
> confronted with a fact that is out of the ordinary,
> does not immediately assume it has occurred because
> the people are ignorant or mistaken, but wonders if
> it really is that way, and what its origins might
> be, and follows up until an answer is found.[14]

This stubborn particularism would naturally tend to resist the master
reform plans of any central bureaucracy.

According to Hashikawa, this does not amount to mere acceptance
of the status quo. Here it is most suggestive to quote directly from
Mannheim on the conservative "counter-utopia," an orientation which
Hashikawa believed Yanagita to share:

> Meaning and reality, norm and existence, are not
> separate here, because the utopia, the "concretized
> idea," is in a vital sense present in this world.
> . . . Although it is true that the utopia, or the
> idea, has become completely congruous with con-
> cretely existing reality, i.e., has been assimilated
> into it, this mode of experience--at least at the
> highest point in the creative period of this current

---

14. Ibid., p. 226; quoting Yanagita, Nihon no matsuri.

--nevertheless does not lead to an elimination of
tensions and to an inert and passive acceptance of
the situation as it is. A certain amount of tension
between idea and existence arises from the fact that
not every element of this existence embodies meaning, and that it is always necessary to distinguish
between what is essential and what is non-essential,
and that the present continually confronts us with
new tasks and problems which have not yet been mas-
tered. . . . But this idea, this spirit, has not
been rationally conjured up and has not been arbi-
trarily chosen as the best among a number of possi-
bilities. It is either in us, as a "silently working force" (Savigny), subjectively perceived, or as
an entelechy which has unfolded itself in the collective creations of the community, of the folk, the
nation, or the state as an inner form which, for the
most part, is perceivable morphologically. The morphological perspective, directed towards language,
art, and the state, develops from that point on.
. . . The approach . . . [is to] follow up the
emanation of "ideas" through the observation of
language, custom, and law, etc., not by abstract
generalizations but rather by sympathetic intuition
and morphological description.[15]

Hashikawa's use of Mannheim here raises at least two questions.
In the first place, one might wonder whether the term "utopian" is
not misapplied to a mode of thought in which meaning and reality are
fundamentally inseparable. Yet as Mannheim points out, there is
still tension in "pure conservatism" between meaningful existence and
existence as such. The conservative idea is selective, never valuing
all existence equally. In this limited, delicate sense, therefore,
it is utopian, and Hashikawa finds this mild form of utopia in Yanagita's thought as well. In the second place, it is necessary to
recognize that the conservative counter-utopia Mannheim saw in Europe
had emerged in reaction to the iconoclastic utopia proffered by bourgeois liberalism: the "liberal-humanitarian idea." The case in Japan
was somewhat different. Yanagita certainly opposed the liberal uni-
versalism of the early-Meiji "enlightenment," but so did the academic/
bureaucratic "regime of truth." Therefore, if we are to argue that

15. Ibid., pp. 231-232; 238. English translation from Karl
Mannheim, Ideology and Utopia, pp. 209-210.

he was anti-establishment, we must show that his conservative counter-utopia reacted not only against bourgeois liberalism but against the kakushin ideas embraced by Japan's bureaucratic leaders. But can the kakushin emphasis on social policy be called "utopian" in a way that would justify the use of the term "counter-utopian" in reference to Yanagita? The answer must be sought in the paradoxical notion of history inherent in the social-policy approach: historical reality, in the form of trends and forces (ikioi, jisei, or taisei), had to be respected, it was thought, but at the same time it was possible through limited intervention to enhance positive aspects of the future society. In sum, whereas Yanagita's "idea" was "counter-utopian" primarily in its selective affirmation of existing reality, the kakushin vision was "utopian" only in its optimistic program of selective modification of the inevitable course of history.

Nevertheless, when recognized as "counter-utopian" even in this limited sense, Yanagita's conservatism takes on the possibility of a critical edge, not only toward the "empty abstractions" of bourgeois liberalism but also with respect to the "renovationist" central bureaucracy, whose "history" was central, elite history and whose interventions were arbitrary from the perspective of the concrete particularities of local customs and conditions. Rather than reforming the country systematically from the center, Yanagita wanted to allow communities and regions to change from within, each according to its own experiences, "prejudices" (Burke) and inner tendencies. Hashikawa points out that, for Yanagita, "the pursuit of the past in the present mediates an opening to the future."[16] Again drawing insight from Mannheim, Hashikawa observes that for bourgeois liberalism the future is everything and the past nothing. (Of course, this was true only to a lesser extent of the kakushin ideology.) The fundamental impetus of conservatism as Yanagita exemplified it, on the

---

16. Hashikawa "Hoshushugi to tenkō," p. 237.

other hand, came from the experience of time, as continuity, which is
the creator of all value.[17]

Hashikawa's essay is one in a series that seeks to probe the war-
time and postwar conversion experiences (tenkō) of Japanese intellectuals. Therefore, he includes an assessment of the degree of consist-
ency apparent in Yanagita's intellectual trajectory through the war
and into the postwar world. Although he concedes the ethical issue
involved in Yanagita's failure actively to resist the war, he concludes that the thrust of Yanagita's scholarship remained precisely
on the track laid down much earlier. Part of his explanation of this
resilient resistance to conversion relies on Yanagita's developed
view of history as not only constant change but endless possibility.
Rather than believing like the literary critic Kobayashi Hideo that
the war transcended history, rendering meaningless all appeals to
relativism, Yanagita retained his sensitivity to the "strange pleni-
tude of the world," and continued to pursue answers to the innumer-
able "questions" (gimon) raised by history as eternal change.[18]

Mountain People and Marginality

Early in his career as a folklorist, while still employed by
the government, Yanagita directed his conservative obsession with
detail toward people who seem to have been on the margins of modern
Japanese society. The first of these works was Tōno monogatari,
tales from a village called Tōno, in Iwate prefecture. In selecting
this topic Yanagita seems merely to have taken an opportunity offered
him by a Tōno local named Sasaki Kyōseki, who told him the legends.
Yet Yanagita quickly recognized their value and after recording them
in an unadorned style, published them himself.

Tsurumi Kazuko has argued that the Tōno collection provides a
critique of the Imperial Rescript on Education (of October 30, 1880),

---

17. Ibid.

18. Ibid., p. 232.

and therefore of the "emperor system" itself, despite Yanagita's
apparent lack of any such intention. She says:

> In a simple, vivid manner, the work demonstrates
> that there existed in the hearts of villagers a set
> of beliefs and norms that were entirely separate
> from emperor worship and the morality of loyalty and
> patriotism that are propounded in the Rescript. In-
> deed, it artlessly demonstrates the total absence of
> such worship and morality.[19]

Tsurumi makes her case as follows. Although the Rescript
preaches filial piety, the Tōno tales tell of the murder of a mother
by her son and the abandonment of the elderly. The Rescript calls
for amity between siblings, but in Tōno a girl kills her elder sister
over potatoes. While the Rescript teaches harmony between spouses,
the stories tell of marital unhappiness, of wives whose babies are
eaten by their husbands, and of women who have the children of frog-
like creatures called kappa. And where the Rescript calls for trust
between friends, the tales tell how a group abandons one of its
number to the wolves.

Second, Tsurumi points out that while the tales are full of
gods (kami) of many types, the kami presented in the Rescript as the
most exalted of all, the emperor, never appears in Tōno. Indeed,
although a distinction is maintained between those who bring good
fortune and those who cause tragedy, there is no perceptible hierarchy among the Tōno deities at all. Therefore, it would appear that
the emperor was not worshipped by the villagers. Indeed,

> If the emperor were recognized as a kami, he would
> clearly be one from outside the community. There-
> fore, for the villagers he would be the object of
> fear, and would be treated in the manner of the
> proverb, "Let sleeping dogs lie."

She concludes:

---

19. Tsurumi Kazuko, "Kaisetsu," in Tsurumi Kazuko, ed., Yanagita Kunio shū, Kindai Nihon shisō taikei 14 (Tokyo: Chikuma Shobo,
1975), p. 443. For a translation of the Tōno monogatari, see Ronald
Morse, tr., Legends of Tōno (Tokyo: The Japan Foundation, 1975).

It had already been twenty years since the propagation of the Rescript. No doubt the people of Tōno
all bowed low before the august imperial portrait
during school ceremonies and the Rescript was
solemnly intoned. Nevertheless, emperor worship
failed to penetrate the hearts of the villagers.
Thus, Tōno monogatari provides us with a crystal
clear view of the posture of resistance by which the
common folk sought to preserve their own beliefs
despite strong pressure from the central government.
That is where I sense Yanagita's own spirit of resistance.[20]

This spirit, according to Tsurumi, is also visible in Yana-

gita's other works on mountain people. The Tōno tales had related

the heritage, not of mountain people, but of ordinary villagers who

lived next to the mountains and therefore mythologized the yamabito

as superhuman kami. Having in Tōno portrayed how the villagers

viewed mountain people, Yanagita then proceeded, in Yamabito gaiden

shiryō (Materials for a Record of Mountain People, 1913-1917), and

Yamabito-kō (A Consideration of Mountain People, 1917), to discuss

the origins of mountain dwellers and in Yama no jinsei (Mountain

Life, 1926) to describe aspects of their life.

By contrasting the yamabito against the settled villagers, whom

he would later designate with the term jōmin, Yanagita clearly demon-

strated their marginal status. Yet he also theorized in Yamabito-kō

that the mountain people were the original inhabitants of Japan, and

that therefore the ancestors of the emperor had actually been con-

querors from outside, presumably from the continent.

Moreover, in the context of a discussion of the various forms

of response adopted by the yamabito's ancestors when they were con-

fronted with the conqueror, Yanagita focuses on the issue of reli-

gion. He speculates that some of the original residents realized

their inability to resist successfully by force, so they adopted a

strategy of outward conformity combined with inner resistance. They

superficially accepted the gods of the conqueror while continuing in

---

20. Tsurumi, "Kaisetsu," p. 446.

private to worship in their traditional manner. Yanagita suggests,
therefore, that what had come to be called "Shinto" was in fact
divided internally between a popular layer (minkan shinkō), representing the traditional beliefs of the conquered people (yamabito),
and a top layer (kokka shintō) that was the religion of the conqueror. The popular layer was concerned, according to Yanagita, with
"seeking constant good fortune throughout all four seasons, day and
night, and trying in a most commonplace way to avoid unease"; its
deities were rustic and natural, "primarily kami of the mountains, of
the wilderness, and of the sea and rivers."[21] The religion of the
conqueror, on the other hand, concentrated its worship on the "divine
origins" of the imperial line.

In an era in which the central government was attempting
through fiat to unify Shinto as a bulwark of the state, Yanagita's
theory of a fundamental split in that belief system was certainly
non-conformist. As Tsurumi readily admits, Yanagita never contested
the emperor system frontally, or "in theory." Nevertheless, he did
cooperate with Minakata Kumagusu in a movement opposing the shrine
consolidation program initiated by the Hara Kei government in 1906.
Yanagita's role was to print and distribute among influential people
the statement of opposition prepared by Minakata. In their major
argument against the measure, they charged that the unification of
Shinto under state sponsorship, and the consolidation of local
shrines would destroy the popular layer of belief which Yanagita had
identified with the original residents of Japan.[22]

In Yamabito-kō, Yanagita speculated that "entering the mountains" (yamairi) had been another of the forms of resistance employed
by original inhabitants when confronted with the conquering society,
and in Yama no jinsei he expanded that notion to cover a variety of
circumstances under which people decided to leave settled society,

---

21. Ibid., p. 227; quoting Yanagita, Yama no jinsei.

22. Ibid., p. 450.

sometimes in protest. He also relates cases which dramatize the extreme poverty and misery that often plagued the lives of mountaineers. With this in mind, Tsurumi argues that "merely to record these concrete examples without interpretation constituted an exposure of the negative side of the existing order."[23]

Yanagita's interest in marginality was continued beyond the yamabito in a study called Kebōzu-kō (1915). Initially intended as an account of itinerant priests (who because of their unshaven heads were called "priests with hair"--kebōzu) this investigation led Yanagita into the problem of the outcaste burakumin. There he advances the hypothesis that discrimination against the burakumin was originally part of a larger problem of all unsettled people (hyōhakumin), a category which included anyone who did not till the land: mountain people, wandering entertainers, religious practitioners of various sorts, artisans, and traveling vendors. Here again, Yanagita called attention to aspects of Japanese society that were inconsistent with the rationalizing, homogenizing aims of the central government. He highlighted not only the variety that pervaded Japanese culture but also the social friction and conflict that formed inescapable dimensions of life.

In at least some of Yanagita's early works, therefore, the dispersive, particularizing tendency that, according to Hashikawa, was inherent in the conservative counter-utopia resulted in an effort to give voice to the marginal, the non-conformist, and the despised in Japanese society.

From "Counter-Utopia" to "Counter-Discipline"

Rather than the mountain people, however, it was the majority of "ordinary" Japanese people in the mainstream of society--the jōmin--on whom Yanagita eventually focused his discipline of Japanese Folklore Studies. Yanagita never rigorously defined the term jōmin,

---

23. Ibid., p. 448.

148

and various viewpoints exist regarding its precise meaning and range
of implication.

Hashikawa provides one view of the jōmin in the context of his
discussion of Yanagita's resistance to ideological conversion. He
says:

> The standards of value in conservative thought were
> "continuity" and "growth." And the ideal it found
> in historical reality was the undifferentiated unit
> (kotai) or national spirit. For Yanagita, the womb
> of that ideal was the existence of the jōmin. Like
> Hegel's "national spirit," the jōmin served as the
> primary storehouse of historical experience, and
> also as a method by which to grasp historical de-
> velopment. . . . The jōmin cherished by Yanagita
> were not an existence given in historical reality
> but a methodological ideal that collected together
> the moments of continuity in the national existence.
> It gave shape to what was eternally constant, and
> its essence was such that change only served to
> expand its compass. It was not a pattern of exper-
> ience related to "status" or "class," but was the
> sort of originary ideal that transcends all institu-
> tions (seido) and temporal determinacy. By nature,
> it tended to view the instrumental qualities of all
> institutions and systems only as alienated forms of
> its own being, and therefore felt no need to respond
> to great institutional changes with anything like a
> "conversion" (tenkō).[24]

By this description, "jōmin" fell somewhere in between an
imposed concept on the one hand and a purely inductive summation of
the concrete particularities of common Japanese experience on the
other. Moreover, as a symbol and vehicle for national continuity,
the jōmin ideal as Hashikawa presents it seems to have been quite
separate from (but perhaps complementary to) symbols such as the
"unbroken imperial line" that were preferred by the Japanese state.

A more specific definition is suggested by Tsurumi based on
Yanagita's statements in a variety of contexts:

> The jōmin are the majority of the Japanese people,
> not the rulers but the ruled; their lives are

---

24. Hashikawa "Hoshushugi to tenkō," p. 239.

conducted according to spoken rather than written
language, they are settled in a particular place,
and they carry on old traditions which they recon-
struct over time through their own ingenuity.[25]

She goes on to schematize Yanagita's mature views in terms of a tri-
adic model that includes the elite, the jōmin and the wanderers:

> In the sense that they are both settled, the jōmin
> and the elite are set apart from the wanderers. But
> members of the elite use not only spoken but written
> language, and therefore not only carry on tradition
> but assimilate foreign culture with great rapidity
> and comprehensiveness. In these aspects, therefore,
> they differ from the jōmin.[26]

Kamishima suggests a more dynamic view of the element jō, which
he defines as the moment of assimilation (as opposed to alienation)
that has operated in Japanese society since the medieval period. He
also emphasizes that the min element of the term is to be seen as
dichotomous to kan, which means "official," but also implies the
values of modernization and Westernization.[27]

In any case, the settled majority of jōmin were made the object
of the "science" of Japanese Folklore Studies when it was conceptualized in the early 1930s. As a research-oriented discipline of social
studies, Minzokugaku had first of all to distinguish itself from
surrounding disciplines such as history, geography, history of religion, and so on. That was accomplished by Yanagita through the radical measure of rejecting written documents as sources. This departure was announced in his Minkan denshō-ron (Popular Legends) of
1934, which has been called the "Declaration of Independence" of

----

25. Ibid., p. 449. A somewhat expanded version of the definition in English appears in Kazuko Tsurumi, "Yanagita Kunio's Work as
a Model of Endogenous Development," Japan Quarterly, Vol. XXII No. 3
(July-September 1975), p. 227.

26. Tsurumi, "Kaisetsu," p. 449.

27. Kamishima, Jōmin no seijigaku, p. 7.

Folklore Studies.[28] It was further elaborated methodologically in
Kyōdo seikatsu no kenkyū-hō (A Method of Studying Local Life) in
1935.

Yanagita outlined a three-tiered method which, if followed,
would eliminate the need for written documentation. The basis for
each tier was provided by the particular form of "folk material"
which was to be collected and studied. The first was the "external
form of life" (seikatsu gaikei), which could be perceived by sight.
This included such elements as clothing, food, lifestyle, houses,
annual observances, and festivals. The second was local "commentary
on life" (seikatsu kaisetsu), or the oral tradition, which had to be
heard to be understood. Here, he included riddles, proverbs, bal-
lads, legends, and so on. The third and "deepest" level was that of
local "life attitudes," or consciousness (seikatsu ishiki), which
could be ascertained neither by sight nor by sound, but had to be
encountered through what Yanagita called kokoro no saishū, or "collection via the heart."[29] Based on the latter portion of Kyōdo
seikatsu no kenkyū-hō, which is not included in the standard edition
of Yanagita's collected works, Tsurumi explains that this included
popular knowledge, or "common sense," a category which was divided
into "life technologies" and "life goals." These, in turn, were to
include not just objective information but value judgments--whether
something was considered good or bad--and also the dimension of why a
certain thing was done, or existed as it did. For practical purposes, the aspect of "life technologies" was centered primarily on
explaining "taboos." Yanagita illustrated it this way:

> When Whites [European ethnologists] narrated studies
> of the lives of Blacks [Africans], they were able to
> make some accurate observations, but with respect to
> these [taboos] they could do nothing. . . . They
> knew that such and such a thing was done, but since

---

28. "Taidan: Yanagita Kunio no gakumon to shisō," in Gotō,
ed., Hito to shisō, p. 27.

29. Yanagita Kunio, Minkan denshōron, in Teihon: Yanagita
Kunio, Vol. 25 (Tokyo: Chikuma Shobo, 1964), p. 336.

it was impossible to reach the inner feelings involved, they were unable to avoid many misunderstandings. Surely someone raised in a different environment could not be expected to understand such things, so with respect to these, at least, it is necessary to rely on natives (kyōdojin) themselves.[30]

As this suggests, Yanagita matched each type of folk material with the sort of researcher who could realistically be expected to study that level. The first category of material could be observed by a casual visitor to an area, while the second, the oral tradition, required at least a considerable period of residence. The third and most important of the three, however, could be studied only by a native. In its most definitive dimension, therefore, Minzokugaku was to consist of a kind of collective introspection carried out by the jōmin themselves.

Written documents played no role in any of the three levels of research, and thus from the outset the method differentiated itself sharply from such documentary disciplines as history. Yanagita believed that it was possible to study the mental phenomena of the past without recourse to written documents because, partly as a result of the rapidity with which Japan had modernized, there was a "past within the present"--not a dead, but a "living" past.[31] Japanese society was layered with "vestiges" and "survivals."[32] He observed that, "In the same hamlet and the same family, people with surprisingly different ways of thinking live together with mutual respect and affection."[33] In his view, this condition provided Japanese folklorists and ethnographers with a unique advantage. It will be apparent, of course, in light of what has already been said

30. Tsurumi, "Kaisetsu," p. 431; quoting Yanagita, Kyōdo seikatsu no kenkyū-hō.

31. Yanagita, Kyōdo seikatsu no kenkyū-hō (abridged), in Teihon, Vol. 25, p. 344.

32. Yanagita Minkan denshōron, in Teihon, Vol. 25, p. 335.

33. Ibid., p. 344.

about Yanagita's conservative sensitivity to continuities between past and present, that this departure represented a happy union between method and philosophical world view.

It is primarily on the basis of the discipline's rejection of written documentation, and Yanagita's criticism of officially-endorsed forms of historiography and Shinto, that Kamishima Jirō has characterized Folklore Studies as the "scholarship of resistance" (teikō no gaku).[34] Yanagita made his most thorough critiques of these modes of learning in two essays written during the Pacific War, Shintō to minzokugaku (Shinto and Folklore Studies, 1943) and Kokushi to minzokugaku (Japanese History and Folklore Studies, 1944). But Yanagita had already set his discipline in a tense relationship with historiography in the Preface to Minkan denshō-ron in 1934, where he noted the limitations of written materials and suggested that the new discipline would provide a kind of non-documentary "supplement" (hojū) to historiography.[35]

It is revealing that in the context of the liberalization of Japanese society following defeat, when "tension" was relaxed, Yanagita returned to the use of written materials in his major postwar studies.[36] This would tend to suggest that there was inherent in the constitutive significance of the rejection of writing, and of the opposition to doctrinal Shinto and academic history it implied, the self-identity of a "counter-discipline" that was to a large extent defined by the function of opposition. Shinto and academic history were not necessarily seen as direct manifestations of the state, although particularly in the case of Shinto that would not have been far from the truth; nor were they even necessarily "symbolic" of the

34. Kamishima, Jōmin no seijigaku, p. 7. Hashikawa uses the term hankō no gaku. See Kamishima Jiro and Itō Mikiharu, eds., Shinpojiumu Yanagita Kunio (Tokyo: NHK, 1973), p. 38.

35. Yanagita, Minkan denshōron, p. 333.

36. Kamishima, Jōmin no seijigaku, p. 7 and Gotō, ed., Hito to shisō, pp. 28-29.

more odious aspects of the militarist state. Yet one could certainly
argue that because of their heavy reliance upon (elite) documents to
legitimize their authority, and the inherent centrism of their con-
structions of Japanese religion and history, they played an important
role in maintaining the "regime of truth" within which the existing
form of the state was made to seem authoritative. If, on the other
hand, true history was accessible neither primarily in the lives of
past elites nor in documentary sources, and if, as Yanagita asserted
in Nihon no matsuri and elsewhere, religious practices were always diverse, to the point that "scriptures play[ed] no role" in Japanese beliefs (see Nussbaum's translation in Part III), then the centralized
state would be deprived of two major intellectual supports for its
claim to be the privileged proprietor of a central stream of tradition. For the state, control of "the book" meant the possibility of
control over culture, and it is here that Yanagita's rejection of
bookish authority took on political significance. Some selections
from his critique of "establishment history" will suggest the thrust
of his "protest." He points implicitly to the narrowly deterministic
implications of exclusive reliance on documentation:

> Even if we leave aside cases in which documents are
> destroyed by fire, it is still true that decisions
> as to what sort of events should be recorded have al-
> ready been made for us by others. Chroniclers, or
> those around them, have made such judgments, and they
> transmit to us only what they find to be worth saving
> or are obliged to save. The right to select is en-
> tirely in their hands. But no matter how sincere
> their intentions, they can have no way of predicting
> what sort of questions will be asked by their descen-
> dants a thousand years hence. . . . Even now, remote
> villages are never visited by anyone who writes.
> Needless to say, therefore, such areas are left out
> of histories based on letters. Even if the residents
> of those undocumented regions were continuously to
> distinguish themselves with extraordinary skills and
> accomplishments, no account of it would ever be in-
> cluded in the historical record. How much less likely,
> then, when they merely go about their uneventful, daily
> lives![37]

---

37. Ienaga Saburō, "Yanagita shigaku-ron," in Gotō, ed., Hito
to shisō, p. 143; quoting Yanagita, Kokushi to minzokugaku, pp. 22-24.

Yanagita argues that the distortive effect of history writing results not only from the bias of its sources but from the chronological distinctions it imposes on the culture of the past:

> Frankly speaking, I do not believe for a moment that, with respect to manners and customs, there are any such chronological divisions as Azuchi-Momoyama. If one admits that these are a mere convenience to aid in explanation or recollection then that is one thing. But it would be outrageous to teach that when Hideyoshi came into power, or right after the center shifted to the regency, a different way of life came into being. . . . I suppose that is what happens when the fruits of research in a culturally-central, urban area are hastily treated like a memorial engraved on behalf of the entire country.[38]

Nevertheless, Yanagita insists, there is an alternative:

> So long as people live in society, and have experienced strong impressions in the past, there will be identifiable remnants of the old ways in various places, even in the midst of the seemingly homogeneous flow of the present. By looking at these we can determine how things were in the past, stretching surprisingly far back. Concerning burials, for example, we have ancient tumuli, and there are even some records from the upper classes. But if one were to write a history implying that these tombs and records represent the way everyone in society buried their dead, surely even the author would be unable to believe it. Yet even today various old ways of preparing the corpse continue to be transmitted, however tenuously. With regard to this kind of problem, a method of proof that employs only a single source of evidence is insufficient. Written documentation has always been scarce and at any rate soon disappears. The representative value of what remains is therefore doubtful. Anyone who tries to write the history of Japanese lamp stands by collecting paintings from picture scrolls (emaki) is bound to fail. Such a study would overlook the stone dishes in which pine is burnt even today, and exclude the lives of those who saw each other's faces only by the light of the hearth.[39]

---

38. Ibid., p. 148.

39. Ibid., p. 145. Also see Tsurumi, "Yanagita's Work as a Model of Endogenous Development," pp. 227-228. Here she quotes Yana-

Yanagita's critique of historical methodology was certainly apposite in view of the heavy emphasis on collection and compilation of documents that characterized standard historical scholarship, particularly that sponsored by the government. Discussing the origins of the government-controlled Ishin Shiryō Hensanjo (Office for the Compilation of Historical Materials on the Restoration), comments by Tōyama Shigeki tend to reinforce Yanagita's point regarding the selection of sources:

> When the proposal for this institution was presented in the Diet, the opposition rejected it, believing it to be a scheme by the Satsuma-Chōshū clique to laud the achievements of their own domains. In response, the government (cabinet of Katsura Tarō, a protege of Yamagita Aritomo) explained that it had no desire to write history, but only to compile "impartially" various types of historical materials "with neither imperial loyalism nor adherence to the position of the shogunate. . . ." And, indeed, by claiming this sort of "impartiality" the government finally did receive offers of historical materials. Yet the nobles, former daimyo, and Elders, who had most of the materials in their possession, kept them closely guarded and revealed only those documents that demonstrated the contributions to the Restoration of their own houses and domains. Thus the prewar scholars of the Meiji Restoration had no choice but to employ as their primary historical sources the biographical writings and compilations contributed in that manner.[40]

The academic histories produced in prewar Japan suffered not only from documentary bias but also from the effect of a variety of official taboos. Indeed, once Japan was at war, the members of official historiographical organs began openly to write history in accord with the imperial myth. In 1938, for example, one year after

gita's postwar evocation of an "icicle model" of social change: "Previous ages are hanging down here and there, like icicles, are they not? . . . In Japan, things changed only like drippings and saggings which are so gradual and slow that it is not easy to discern when they changed, if they changed at all." Daini Yanagita taidan shū (Tokyo: Chikuma Shobo, 1965), pp. 65-57.

40. Tōyama, Meiji ishin to gendai, pp. 16-17.

the Marco Polo Bridge Incident, the Ishin Shiryō Hensanjo abandoned
its "objective" compilation of documents and began work on two writing projects to commemorate the "2,600th anniversary of the founding
of the nation." The results were the Gaikan ishinshi (Outline of the
History of the Restoration) and the six-volume Ishin-shi (History of
the Restoration).[41] By orienting his discipline to the jōmin and
approaching the national level only from the "bottom up," Yanagita
seems to have avoided the extremities of jingoism, although of course
one can argue along with Bernier (in this volume) that many of Yanagita's wartime concerns paralleled the centrally-imposed myths of
kokutai.

The materialist historiography produced by Marxists beginning
in the late-1920s certainly raised the scientific level of the discipline, particularly with respect to the Meiji Restoration. Nevertheless, from the perspective of Yanagita's critique, the "scientific," documentary approach of the Marxists, and even their careful
albeit often abstract attention to the historical role of the masses,
did not suffice to differentiate their work fundamentally from that
of the establishment academics. To the extent that it focused on the
conventions of documentation and historical methodology, therefore,
Yanagita's counter-discipline was at least as anti-Marxist as it was
anti-establishment.

Ancestor Worship and "Invisible History"

If Minzokugaku can plausibly be called a "scholarship of resistance," therefore, it is not because it openly opposed the state or
its policies, but rather because there was built into its very constitution as a discipline a radical posture of disbelief with respect
to the documents, objectives, and methods that formed the basis of
authority in the academic and religious establishments. It suggested
a different way of thinking about history and culture, one which
might have encouraged an attitude of skepticism toward the overly

---

41. Ibid., p. 17.

centralized and homogenized representation of the past sponsored by the state.

Minzokugaku opened up a new cultural space, a panoramic slice of Japanese life, that claimed its own history, actors, and forms of belief. This space was represented most concretely in the category of the jōmin, which was defined primarily by the absence of written culture. The absence of writing, in turn, provided this space with a measure of autonomy from culture as it had been constituted by the elite, in government and academia.

Perhaps the most interesting general conception of how the cultural realm of the jōmin is related to that of the elite can be traced to the late-Tokugawa nativist, Hirata Atsutane (1776-1843). In the context of a discussion of where souls go after death, Hirata distinguished this life from the next in terms of a contrast between "visible world" (utsushiyo) and "invisible world" (kakuriyo). He concluded that the latter, the world of the dead, was ruled by the deity Ōkuninushi-no-mikoto and was centered in Izumo, while the former, the world of the living, was governed by the descendants of Amaterasu Ōmikami. There is an obvious parallel between this conception and Yanagita's distinction, in Yamabito-kō, between state Shinto, which focused worship on Amaterasu, and the popular Shinto of Japan's original inhabitants, the yamabito. Moreover, the basic structure of this dichotomy also seems to fit Yanagita's contrast between the jōmin, forgotten and therefore "invisible," and the elite whose visible, public history is presented as "Japan's" history.

According to Tsurumi, the strongest link between Yanagita's Minzokugaku and Hirata's Kokugaku (nativism) is provided by Yanagita's interpretation of Japanese ancestor worship. Here, of course, a basic text is Senzo no hanashi (About Our Ancestors), where Yanagita presents a view of the proximity between the worlds of the living and the dead that is similar to Hirata's. Yanagita makes the connection explicit:

Interest in the problem of Yūmei-do (afterworld) by
Japanese scholars is of such a recent date that we
could say it started with Hirata Atsutane. . . .

He goes on to mention his own early education in the Hirata school of
Kokugaku:

Matsuura Shūhei [a teacher of Hirata Kokugaku],
under whom I studied, was one of those believers.
Even though we cannot see, there is a concealed
world between you and me. What we say is always
heard by somebody. What we do is seen by somebody.[42]

The possibility of a continual intermingling between the living
and the dead is fundamental to this cosmology, setting it in opposition to popular Buddhist conceptions of a Hell, or other world far
away. Summing up various aspects of what he believed to be the pre-
Buddhist Japanese view, he says:

If we were to present at least four conspicuously
Japanese elements, the first would be the view that
souls remain in their country after death instead of
going off far away; the second would be the idea
that there are goings and comings between the two
worlds, the clear and the dark, and at other than
fixed occasions of spring and autumn there were
times when the living invited, could invite, the
souls; the third would be the idea that the dying
wish of the living could be carried out and he could
make all sorts of plans for his descendants; and the
fourth would be the idea that he could be reborn
again and again to carry on in his same work. These
articles of belief were eventually very important,
but since they did not belong to an organized
religion, they were not handed down in writing, and
there was no way for people to identify their ideas
with those of others, causing small differences to
arise among them.[43]

Drawing on the tone of solidarity across generations that is
evident in this and other passages, Tsurumi postulates an "invisible

---

42. Yanagita Kunio, About Our Ancestors, tr. by Fanny Hagin
Meyer and Ishiwara Yasuyo (Tokyo: Ministry of Education, 1970), p.
147.

43. Ibid., p. 146.

history" among the jōmin which, through the medium of tasks and hopes
that are passed down over great periods of time, links ancestors, the
living, and future generations. This is a "history of frustration,
an invisible history," because a single individual or family can
never realize their hopes in one lifetime. But these are taken up by
their descendants, and might be realized eventually. Here, then, ancestor worship links up with Yanagita's "conservative" definition of
history as a past within the present, and also with his conception of
the jōmin:

> What Yanagita calls "ancestors," or "the other
> world," is a body of accumulated tradition. It is
> the totality of latent possibilities formed by the
> projects attempted in the past but not completed.
> . . . The past is actualized as possibility for the
> present and the future. Yanagita also suggests that
> the past is not fixed, but able to be recon-
> structed.[44]

The cultural space opened up by Yanagita includes, therefore,
not only a category of people defined by their unlettered state, but
a "history" of ancestor-worship that links the jōmin with the world
of the dead. Through such a linkage the jōmin themselves symboli-
cally become an ontological entity analogous to Hirata's "invisible
realm"; it is their history of darkness and frustration, therefore,
that sets the jōmin apart from the elite, urban culture of "visible"
Japan.

So far, this assimilation of Yanagita's jōmin to Hirata's
kakuriyo does little more than provide us with a richer image of the
profound degree of separateness and autonomy that might be attributable to the world of the "hidden" jōmin. But with respect to the
potential for resistance, what is most interesting about the comparison with Hirata is its implication not merely of autonomy but of
superiority. For Hirata, the two worlds were by no means equal. The
visible world was only temporary, preparatory stage prior to entrance into the hidden underworld ruled by Ōkuninushi. Moreover,

---

44. Tsurumi, "Kaisetsu," p. 454.

although that world is invisible from the perspective of the living, the world of the living is clearly visible from the world of the dead. The souls of the dead can not only see everything that transpires in the visible world but also see far into its future.[45] There is little room for doubt, therefore, that by appealing to Hirata's dichotomy Yanagita seeks to imply not merely parity but the clear priority of the jōmin culture over that of the elite.

When considered further, it becomes evident that this sort of reversal, by which a secondary or marginal entity is claimed to be equal or even primary, is typical of Yanagita's general value orientation. He believed that women, children, and the elderly were the "bearers of old customs and unconscious tradition" and he therefore insisted that they merited special attention from folklorists (see Yamashita's paper in this volume). Moreover, we have seen that in his early work on mountainfolk Yanagita implicitly raised their status vis-à-vis the settled majority by postulating that they were the original inhabitants of Japan and that their religious tradition was autonomous from the officially-sponsored state Shinto. Even after he shifted the focus of his work to the jōmin majority, he continued via the discipline of Minzokugaku to put common culture on a par with that of the elites.

Yet Yanagita's affinity for the marginal and secondary rather than the central and primary was not merely a matter of values. It was also a matter of polemical strategy. Yanagita could most convincingly establish the logical and rhetorical basis for his discipline by making it the antithesis of what he took to be the elite, bureaucratic paradigm for scholarship. Here, it is important to recognize that Yanagita's fledgling "counter-discipline" appeared only after the state, the "emperor system," and the kakushin form of bureaucratic rule were already preeminent. This was the case because, as Mannheim pointed out with respect to Europe,

---

45. Sakurai Tokutarō, "Yanagita Kunio no sosenkan," in Tsurumi, ed., Yanagita Kunio shū, p. 423.

Conservative mentality as such has no predisposition towards theorizing. This is in accord with the fact that human beings do not theorize about the actual situations in which they live as long as they are well adjusted to them. They tend . . . to regard the environment as part of a natural world-order which, consequently, presents no problems. Conservative mentality as such has no utopia.[46]

Therefore, the conservative counter-utopia and its scholarly apparatus are formed only as "a means of self-orientation and defense" in the face of aggression against the natural order. In a pattern reminiscent of Hegel's famous "owl of Minerva," Yanagita's conservative discipline took flight in Japan only after power and "truth" were firmly in the grip of the kakushin bureaucratic elite. It was therefore reactive in form.

That is why Yanagita described the popular space of the jōmin by contrasting it against the advanced culture of writing; the naive matsuri of the people in opposition to the systematized state Shinto of the modernizing elite (see translation in Part III); and the "round" language of the people against the "square" language of the intellectuals (see Ōiwa's paper). Indeed, the object of research (non-elite) of Minzokugaku, the source materials (non-written) that were to be used, and the type of researcher to be employed (non-outsider, i.e., native) were all defined as the opposite of their equivalents in such modernized disciplines as orthodox history and Shinto.

Moreover, when Yanagita uses such oppositions to describe substantive differences, as in his contrast between sairei and matsuri in the translation in Part III of this volume, or between mai and odori, or hanashi and katari, as described by Ōiwa's paper, there is never any doubt as to which term of the dichotomy Yanagita believed to be the more "authentic" and thus primary. He was equally partial with respect to methodological oppositions, such as that between written as opposed to non-written materials, although with them he

---

46. Mannheim, Ideology and Utopia, pp. 206-207.

was sometimes less explicit. As noted above, he originally described Minzokugaku as a discipline that would "supplement" those that relied on documents. Later, however, he admitted his view that the true motive force of history is the jōmin rather than the elite,[47] implying that Minzokugaku itself was the primary discipline while conventional historiography, which studied only the elite, could be only supplementary.

Inasmuch as such dichotomies formed both the methodological foundation and substantive pillars of the discipline of Folklore Studies, it would seem difficult to deny its critical implications. It was by definition a "counter-discipline" whose methods and categories for the delineation and explanation of reality were all chosen in such a way as to counteract directly those employed by the more conventional disciplines. In that respect, it was at least indirectly subversive of the modern Japanese academic and bureaucratic order.

At the same time, we are forced to recognize that insofar as Minzokugaku originally defined itself in opposition to the existing "regime of truth," it remained, ironically, not only somewhat similar to that regime (see Bernier's paper), but conceptually dependent upon it. In the absence of a coercively centralizing and modernizing establishment, neither a conservative "counter-utopia" nor a "counter-discipline" makes much sense. Hence the restructuring (not, by any means, the complete elimination) of major aspects of the prewar regime in the wake of World War II also weakened the raison d'etre of Folklore Studies as a coherent discipline. In this connection, Yanagita's apparent return to the use of written materials after the war is indeed provocative. He seems, in effect, to have abandoned the defining tenet of his discipline as soon as basic aspects of the establishment it opposed began to be transformed. As Ronald Morse

---

47. Yanagita, "Nihon rekishi kandan," Yanagita Kunio taidan shū, (Tokyo: Chikuma Shobō, 1964), pp. 185, 189. For an extended quote, see Tsurumi, "Yanagita's Work as a Model of Endogenous Development," pp. 225-226.

has observed, by the time Yanagita died in 1962, "The study of folk-lore, as such, had lost its sense of unity and focus."[48]

Yet while the institution of Minzokugaku atrophied, its counter-utopian idea took on new life. In the years following the disillusionment with "postwar democracy" that accompanied the struggle against the revised Japan-U.S. Security Treaty in 1960,[49] it again became apparent to some intellectuals that bureaucratic centralism, urban elitism, and a kakushin establishment--the latter now centered on the Socialist and Communist parties and the Sōhyō federation of national unions--were again firmly entrenched. One of the results of this realization was the rediscovery of Yanagita's conservative counter-utopia by many who were disenchanted with both bureaucratic modernization and the established kakushin left.

The renewed interest in Yanagita's perspective, which was taken to imply such elements as emphasis on the common, small and marginal, a sensitivity to particularity and diversity, respect for community, and a spirit of opposition to modernizing elites, was not accompanied by a comparable resurgence in the "counter-discipline" of Minzoku-gaku. Now, however, Yanagita attracted influential supporters in other disciplines: Tada Michitarō and Tsurumi Kazuko in sociology, Kamishima Jirō in political science, Yamamoto Kenkichi in literary criticism, Yoneyama Toshinao and Itoh Mikiharu in anthropology, and the late Hashikawa Bunsō in intellectual history.

Perhaps the postwar fate of Folklore Studies can best be summarized in a final appeal to the Hegelian idiom favored by Mannheim and Hashikawa: Minzokugaku was dialectically overcome (aufgehoben)--terminated as a discipline in order to be preserved as a frame of mind and orientation to scholarship. If so, one could argue further that the catalyst of that dialectical movement, central to the moment

48. Ronald A. Morse, "Personalities and Issues in Yanagita Kunio Studies," Japan Quarterly, Vol. XXII No. 3 (July-September 1975), p. 249.

49. See George R. Packard III, Protest in Tokyo (Princeton, NJ: Princeton University Press, 1961).

of demise as well as that of rebirth, was the reactive, oppositional structure that had been inherent in Yanagita's discipline from the beginning.

PART III

A TRANSLATION

THE EVOLUTION OF JAPANESE FESTIVALS: FROM MATSURI TO SAIREI

Yanagita Kunio

INTRODUCTION AND TRANSLATION

Stephen Nussbaum

Nihon no Matsuri is one of Yanagita Kunio's best known works.
It comprises a series of lectures given at Tokyo University in the
fall of 1941. The following translation is the second of its seven
chapters and deals with the major shift Yanagita sees in the development of Japan's indigenous religious traditions. Although the term
matsuri is frequently translated as "festival," Yanagita quickly
warns us that we would be amiss in viewing this as a treatise on
Japan's major festivals such as the well known one at the Gion Shrine
in Kyoto. Rather, it is an exploration of a faith and sentiment indigenous to Japan--one which is inextricably woven in rituals and
only knowable through participation in them. Matsuri refers to these
indigenous rites. Thus, in addition to The Festivals of Japan, the
title of this work could be translated as The Religious Rites of
Japan or even Japanese Religion.

It is a classic in the study of Japanese religion and as such
has established the tone and many of the themes and interpretations
appearing in subsequent works on Japanese festivals. It is also a
classic in what has lately been dubbed nihonjinron (theories of being
Japanese). In many ways Yanagita's prime concern has become the
quintessential issue for many twentieth century Japanese intellectuals: the search for a Japanese sense of selfhood or identity in a
world characterized by a sudden and forced acknowledgment of cultural
diversity.

167

Unlike many of his contemporaries and successors, however, Yanagita sought this in neither classical texts nor moral aphorisms. He also avoids the seemingly fashionable psychological and sociological reductionisms. Rather he looked for the meaning of being Japanese in the multifaceted ebb and flow of daily life.

His approach to doing this is hard to classify, but his immediate goal is clear. It is the discovery of a unity of belief and sentiment in a plurality of ritual forms. In the following pages he states that a rigorous attempt at establishing such a unity has never been made and that because this belief has no textual or scriptural basis its nature is far from obvious. He felt that given the powerful forces at work in the modern world the unity of matsuri was in danger of being lost or exploited. Accordingly in the following pages Yanagita has given himself the political task of bridging the gap between an oral religion of sentiment and rite and the demands both of the modern world and the written word. He is sensitive to the dilemma in which this places him and his response to it speaks to a number of contemporary concerns in the social sciences.

There are at least three levels on which one may approach this text: as a seminal work on Japanese religion, as an important interpretation of Japanese culture, and finally as a study in method.

Regarding the first of these, in examining matsuri throughout the country Yanagita discovers several common, though often masked, forms. These include a period of ritual abstinence preceding a matsuri, the demarcation of an area for performing matsuri, the descent of the gods to such grounds, and their entertainment there as honored guests. He is interested, however, not only in discovering these forms, but also in tracing their development through time. In doing this he shares an important assumption with many nineteenth and early twentieth century scholars. This concerns the interchangeability of geography and history, the notion that one may travel back in time by moving spatially toward the hinterland. According to this way of thought the city is an important locus of cultural change and the entire country becomes a living museum. This permits one personally to observe rites originating at different times in the past and, by contrasting them, to establish their approximate chronology.

While Yanagita was clearly concerned with reconstructing the past and outlining the stages in the development of matsuri, it should be noted that he did not see his job as simply uncovering ancient practices. Nor does he feel that such practices are necessarily "better" or more valuable than contemporary ones. Rather he states that the sentiment which envigorates matsuri is found in both newer and older ritual forms and is known to many contemporary Japanese. He sees his countrymen throughout their history as being intrinsically inquisitive and their common life as an evolving drama. In a sense, Levi-Strauss's metaphor of the bricoleur is an appropriate way of viewing the relation between the Japanese and their matsuri. They are continually working with and changing their forms while investing them with a unity which is deeper than any of its expressions.

Through time, however, a distance has been placed between many Japanese and the rites they watch and perform. Yanagita's response to this increasing secularization of matsuri is part of his response to the national identity crisis mentioned earlier. In both cases he is concerned with the threatened character of meaning--a concern similar to many Western existentialists. He differs from them, however, in that rather than viewing the individual as creating his own essence, he sees us as discovering one in an on-going stream of language and action. His personal and political goal then is to invigorate this stream so that it might continue as a viable mirror of identity for all Japanese. Its study, while rigorous, consequently can be neither neutral nor fully objective.

It should also be noted that in arguing that the webs of significance structuring matsuri possess a common form he is not suggesting that they can be reduced to a common core, at least not a core which can be easily summarized in the written word as in a statement of essential values. Rather, his archaeology of contemporary ritual turns on a distinction between domains or types of religious discourse. He draws this distinction at the very beginning of the following text and summarizes it in an opposition between shinkō (belief or faith) and shūkyō (religion). Both of these are found in Japan, the former referring to indigenous religious traditions and the latter to religious traditions such as Buddhism or Christianity. He sees these areas of religious discourse as organized along different lines and accordingly necessitating different modes of analysis.

Religions have a textual basis and a central authority which dictates uniform practices. This sets them off from the domain of matsuri and reverberates a key distinction in all of Yanagita's work, that between history, the record of the elite, and minzokugaku (his field of study), the record of the common person. On a political level this echoes a distinction between outside authority and local autonomy. From an indigenous perspective then, religions possess a uniformity which violates both the local autonomy of ritual and belief and the autonomy of a non-discursive mode of knowledge. One favored way Yanagita refers to these differing realms of discourse is in stating that a primitive person (genshijin) still lives within every Japanese. This primitive person is the realm of the autonomous self and is the domain his analysis is attempting to penetrate.

The method Yanagita employs repeatedly in the following pages is inductive and contextual. His concern is with the immediately tangible signs--both linguistic and physical--of religious experience. He explores them by mapping them within the context of the living museum. In doing this he is sensitive to the manner in which regional and national contexts influence local matsuri. And he links developments in matsuri to diverse currents of change including political centralization, urbanization, nationalism and an evolving technology.

One final note. Many Japanese readers find the logic of Yanagita's writings to be difficult to follow but rich in reverberations.
This means that it is frequently long after one has read him that
unanticipated meanings emerge. In general his prose is suggestive
rather than conclusive--as is appropriate to his goal of mediating
between something which has never been said and is not a product of
discursive thought and the demands of the written word. In this way,
his method of writing incorporates rather than objectifies his topic.
This makes for a challenging translation and results in a text which
may require some patience on the part of the English reader. In
trying to maintain the form of the original I have kept its divisions, both into sections and into paragraphs. Finally, the following treatise may leave the reader attuned to the western sociology of
religion unsatisfied. He would be well advised to look elsewhere for
a discussion of the multiple functions of religion in Japanese society. Those interested in an original exploration of the immediate
signs of religious experience should find Yanagita's work insightful
and provocative.

From <u>Matsuri</u> to <u>Sairei</u>[1]

i

Now, in six lectures, I would like to discuss the festivals of
Japan. In Japan, without coming to grips with these observances,
known as <u>matsuri</u>, it is impossible to come to know both the old forms
of our country's unique beliefs and those changing conditions which
have resulted in their present altered appearances. I am sure the
reasons for this can be quickly discerned by students such as you.
Today, when you compare any of the religious organizations known as
the great religions (for example, Buddhism or Christianity) with our

---

1. <u>matsuri kara sairei e</u> 祭から祭礼へ . This is chapter
two of <u>Nihon no Matsuri</u> 「日本の祭」 by Yanagita Kunio 柳田國男 .

indigenous traditions, it quickly becomes apparent that scriptures
play no role in our beliefs. At most, there are some people who feel
that parts of our country's officially approved history should cor-
respond to sacred works.[2] Not only, however, have the vast majority
of our country's most loyal believers never had the opportunity to
read these works, but they have never been taught their beliefs
through books. Consequently, there have never been any preachers
and, at the very least, in our everyday life--when matsuri are not
being held--there has never been any proselytizing. And, as I will
attempt to explain, in earlier times there were no professional
priests, let alone any fraternal religious associations. Although it
is true that each shrine had several leaders, their teaching was to
be conveyed exclusively by their conduct and sensibilities; on normal
days and occasions they would be hesitant to mention anything dealing
with matsuri. In other words, such knowledge was to be acquired only
by those who regularly renewed their experience of matsuri by participating in several each year. The rotation of the four seasons is,
in temperate countries, a very convenient aid for remembering things.
Our matsuri have taken this as a signal and through it have been repeated since ancient times. Not participating in a matsuri has always been seen as a great misfortune and at times it has even been
felt that such negligence was difficult to condone. Accordingly,
matsuri have, in a sense, always been a single line of stepping
stones forming the religious bond of the Japanese people. This means
that by treading any other path it would have been impossible for a
person to have understood Kannagara no Michi, or the ancient way of
the gods.[3]

   Today ordinary people still understand most of the ancient
meaning of the Japanese term matsuri; they recognize its essential

---

   2. This is a reference to the Kojiki 「古事記」 compiled
in 712 A.D., and the Nihon Shoki 「日本書紀」, compiled in 720
A.D.

   3. 惟神之道 This is a pseudonym for Shintō.

aspects and know how broadly it may be applied. There is no reason for those who, since their childhood, have never missed even one of the yearly repetitions of matsuri to make a mistake in using this term. While many would probably be perplexed if they were asked to express the meaning of "matsuri" in a concise, definition-like sentence, those who have used this word countless times throughout their lives all know what a matsuri is and what it is not. If it were ever used incorrectly, the listener would, at the very least, be somewhat puzzled. In recent times, people who live in cities and those who have only rarely attended matsuri have sometimes attempted to explain this term.[4] Because of this, things have become somewhat confused and the general idea of matsuri can no longer be clearly formulated.

ii

One problem we might take up in order to clarify this situation concerns whether matsuri and sairei are the same or different. A hasty person would probably quickly conclude that sairei is a fancy expression for "matsuri." In reality, however, there are many "matsuri" which no one would call "sairei." For example, when someone builds a house, a "ridgepole raising matsuri,"[5] is conducted. And after cleaning a well one offers a matsuri to the god of the well. Such things are certainly not sairei. If we pursue this matter a little further, when one becomes apprehensive about his family, or

---

4. During much of Yanagita's lifetime the government attempted to use religion as a means of social control. See Daniel C. Holtom, Modern Japan and Shinto Nationalism: A Study of Present-day Trends in Japanese Religions, Chicago, University of Chicago Press, 1947.

5. muneage no matsuri 棟上げの祭 . This is one of several rituals performed during the construction of a house. It is performed by the carpenter in conjunction with the erection of a house's frame or supporting pillars. During it, he places offerings before the gods, pays homage to the deities of the four directions and erects the frame. This is followed by a communal feast. In some areas an arrow is placed pointing in the direction of the house's "unlucky corner" (kimon 鬼門 literally, "demon's gate") or offerings are made of women's hair and combs.

sees something in a dream and has his fortune told, he is sometimes informed that there have not been enough "matsuri" for his ancestors. Even when those rituals which are today referred to in Buddhist terminology, such as "memorial service"[6] or "the appeasement of spirits having no descendants,"[7] are expressed in indigenous terms, they are "matsuri." On the other hand, even those sairei at which the term "sairei" is written on the banners and hanging lanterns are referred to by women and children simply as "matsuri" or "omatsuri."[8] In the Tōhoku region there are still many villages in which the word "sairei" is not used. In such areas it is only among a few of the more educated people that expressions such as "gosharei"[9] have occasionally been used referring to large matsuri. Even though the characters with which sairei is written literally refer to the "ceremony" of a "matsuri," when "matsuri" and "sairei" are spoken they sound like two completely different things. Accordingly those who feel these terms are not synonymous with each other are more accurate. In its popular usage, one could probably define a sairei as a matsuri, but one which is particularly beautiful and gay and has many enjoyable facets. More concretely, a sairei could also be thought of as a matsuri at which many spectators gather; this formulation, however, is incomplete in that just what constitutes a

---

6. hoji 法事 . A general term referring to Buddhist memorial services. It usually does not refer to the funeral ceremony, but rather to those services which, during the first year following a person's death, are held every month on the day of death and after that are held every year on the date of death. Such services are conducted by a Buddhist priest and are attended by the friends and close relatives of the deceased. They are generally followed by a communal meal.

7. bonsegaki 盆施餓鬼 .

8. オマツリ . The initial "o" is a widely used honorific prefix.

9. ゴシャレイ (御社礼) . This term would probably be written with the characters in parentheses, meaning a rite or ceremony performed at a shrine.

"spectator"[10] must still be explained. Although "sairei" was originally a foreign word and there is no reason for it to have been in
Japan since early times, it, nevertheless, can be found in the records of the people of Kyoto as early as the Kamakura period. It was
probably in use somewhat before that time, but from the beginning was
not merely another expression for matsuri, rather it seems to have
been used only in reference to the large matsuri of famous shrines;
in other words, the old usage of this word is largely synonymous with
its current meaning.

Three problems arise in connection with this. The first is:
until "sairei" was imported or recast in Japan, by what term was this
distinction between sairei and other matsuri expressed in the different parts of the country? Or, on the other hand, was there originally no need for such a distinction? Even today, when one carefully
looks through official documents it seems that the term "sairei" is
not used very often. Instead, "grand matsuri"[11] is used by most
people with the meaning of sairei. That is, among the dozens of
matsuri held each year, only one is large enough and sufficiently
well known to be commonly referred to as a "grand matsuri." Was not
this word possibly also found in olden times, originally being termed
"ōmatsuri"[12] and currently "taisai?"[13] I feel that the distinction
between "matsuri" and "omatsuri" may also be related to this. While
among women there already seems to be confusion regarding these
latter two terms, some men still differentiate between them. A particularly unusual case is to be seen in the matsuri occurring in the
eleventh month at the Kasugawakamiya Shrine in Nara. This is, with-

---

10. kenbutsu 見物 .

11. taisai 大祭 .

12. オホマツリ . This is an alternative reading for taisai.

13. See note 11.

out doubt, popularly known as "onmatsuri."[14] No one refers to it simply as "matsuri." It is likely that originally there was something significant in the usage of these honorifics. Namely, since some matsuri were carried out by aristocrats rather than by one's group, they were referred to as "omatsuri"--only those which were performed on a small autonomous basis were simply referred to as "matsuri." However, since it was easy to confuse these terms, this situation may have resulted in a very small number of matsuri coming to be called "sairei." There may also be people who maintain that the distinction between "matsuri" and "sairei" relates to a difference between official and private matsuri. However, since on a national basis many shrines have sairei while very few receive official matsuri emissaries, it appears that originally there was no official-private distinction. Initially, probably only large and small matsuri were distinguished at each shrine, and, as might be expected, it was probably later that it became fashionable for the larger ones to be attended by the court aristocracy.

If this supposition is acceptable, then our second problem requires that we explain the differences between large and small matsuri. Put in a different way, what could have necessitated the use of a new word, "sairei," to set off those matsuri to which it refers from other more general matsuri? In line with this, given all the matsuri occurring each year, what caused the gradual increase in areas having only one "grand matsuri?" For sure, one could broadly state that such changes spring from the evolving character of the world. This in turn leads us to an explanation of how the changing world has influenced all of the different facets of our matsuri.

----

14. オンマツリ . The initial "on" is an honorific prefix. For a brief discussion of its derivation consult R. A. Miller, The Japanese Language, p. 276.

iii

The third problem is an even more fundamental one. Namely, if
sairei are a certain kind of matsuri, and if the term "matsuri" has
not been forgotten since early times, then there must be an important
common dimension joining all of these matsuri; yet how should one go
about uncovering it? Our matsuri have been influenced by the culture
of various periods, and their appearances have changed along with the
world. Moreover, in that they have developed independently at each
shrine, matsuri, and particularly sairei, differ greatly in their external appearances. One therefore must search on a more basic level
for their fundamental common features. Fortunately, the very circumstances which I have just mentioned facilitate our discovery of this
underlying dimension. This is because if matsuri were, like the
ritual beliefs of Buddhists, decided for the entire country, fixed
and taught according to the religion or the sect, then, to the extent
that accurate records were not kept, it would be difficult to recon-
struct an earlier practice. Old examples of matsuri are, however,
found at each shrine, and accordingly the diverse steps in their
development are preserved. In addition to this, various isolated
innovations can also be discovered. And, although we have by now
grown used to them, very extensive variations can be found sometimes
even within the matsuri and sairei of a single area. Taken as manifestations of one belief, one about which doubts have never been
entertained, these are merely an example of an implicit faith born
among the Japanese people; if, however, an outsider were to view this
multiplicity of forms it would only be natural for him to be skep-
tical about their underlying unity. This ambiguous situation should
not be left forever as it is.

Of these three problems, we must naturally expend most of our
efforts on the last one and attempt to uncover those features which
are shared by all of our matsuri. So far as method is concerned,
however, it is convenient for us to approach this final problem
through a consideration of the second one, of the distinction between

large and small _matsuri_. Even though it has been reported that there
are some shrines at which there are as many as fifty to seventy matsuri a year for their guardian deities,[15] when we think of _matsuri_ we
usually think of _sairei_, of the spectacles we watched wide-eyed as
children. Nowadays, however, when one is walking in the country and
sees a quiet, simple observance at a small shrine, he is likely to
feel that it is probably a _matsuri_ but that its participants are poor
and are intentionally simplifying it by carrying out its barest out-
lines. Another viewpoint, however, also exists. According to it,
sairei were the result of a lot of planning and additions of new attraction to these simple observances, making them into showy pag-
eants. In reality it is the latter of these two viewpoints which is
more warrantable.

Let me give a few examples so that my lecture will be more
readily understood. When _sairei_ is mentioned, most people think of
different kinds of hanging lanterns, for example. No one could help
but experience the feeling of a _matsuri_ in being soothed by the scene
of long paper lanterns dangling from the eaves of every neighborhood
during the _sairei_ of a community such as Takayama in Hida. If one
delves more deeply into this association of hanging lanterns with
sairei additional questions come to mind. For example, when did
candles first come to Japan? How long has paper been widely available? How long have the techniques been available for applying this
paper to finely bent bamboo slivers so that it may freely expand and
contract? Or how long have techniques been available for painting
such paper with paulownia oil so that even if it becomes wet it will
not fall apart? Without the combination of these two techniques
there could have been no hanging lanterns, yet even before their

---

15. Such deities are associated not only with a shrine but
also with the locality in which it is found. All of those living
within the area are traditionally considered to be "filial" to this
deity. For a discussion of the meaning of the term "kami" 神 which
is here translated as "deity," "deities," "god," or "gods" see D. C.
Holtom, "The Meaning of Kami" in _Monumenta Nipponica_, 3 (1940), pp.
1-27, 392-413, and 4 (1941), pp. 25-68.

diffusion there were <u>matsuri</u> in this country. Actually, even now the light coming from bonfires and torches is used in the nighttime portions of some <u>matsuri</u>; in certain regions names of <u>matsuri</u> even come from characteristics such as these.

iv

Another scene frequently associated with <u>sairei</u> is the fluttering of banners in the autumn wind over rice paddies. These are made from a bolt of white cloth with loops attached along its sides. A pole has been passed through these and upon the cloth petitions are written in large characters for such things as "the safety of our land"[16] or "a plentiful harvest of the five cereals."[17] In that I have yet to find any traces of such banners in medieval scrolls or records it seems that they have become popular only fairly recently. I plan to deal with this problem in more detail in a later lecture, but I might mention here that while there is no doubt but that the role played by these banners dates from the very beginning of <u>matsuri</u> in Japan, the form in which they now appear is completely different from that of earlier times.

An even more general characteristic of <u>sairei</u> has been the ceremonial carrying of portable shrines and the many beautiful processions which accompany such shrines. Since early medieval times these processions have, in Kyoto and other places, been referred to as "the newly elegant."[18] This "new elegance" was centered about an impulsive competition in new designs and a yearly changing in the

16. <u>kokudo anzen</u> 国土安全 .

17. <u>gokoku jōju</u> 五穀成就 . The five traditional crops of Japan are rice, barley, foxtail millet, beans, and Chinese millet. Some lists include <u>hie</u> 稗 a Deccan grass.

18. <u>furyū</u>. A term with many different shadings of meanings which has often captured the imagination of the Japanese. It literally refers to the wind and the flow of a stream or river, and is here translated as "the newly elegant" or "creative splendor."

appearance of a matsuri. It could even be said that this caused our
matsuri to become sairei. Although I feel that the descent of the
gods to the matsuri grounds reflects an old way of thinking, the
glittering golden portable shrines we see nowadays with which they
are received and carried jingling about an area are found only at
larger matsuri. It seems likely that vestiges of these developments
are to be found even among the historical records of the sairei of
Kyoto and its surrounding areas. Although the use of a horse to
welcome the gods to the matsuri grounds is older than that of vehicles such as portable shrines (and is still now fairly widespread),
there are also early examples of such shrines. One example from
medieval history is the portable shrine of the famous Hiyoshi Shrine,
another is the divine branch of the Kasugawakamiya Shrine which was
carried about on a small shrine or platform held at waist level by
two men. Originally, decorated portable shrines, like the ones becoming popular today, were found only at a limited number of shrines.
We assume that the Gion Shrine in Kyoto was probably the first of
these. If, however, we look at shrines where the history of their
matsuri is known, such as the Goryō and the Imamiya Shrines, we can
go on to state that it appears only those matsuri performed especially in order to placate the anger of the terrifying gods were
planned to be as beautiful as possible. At any rate, there is no
doubt but that at most shrines throughout the country these beautiful
portable shrines began to be used in the passage of the gods as
vehicles which were both fashionable and innovational. This occurred
during the peaceful period following the sixteenth century, and accordingly, these portable shrines first became popular in basically
urban areas. These developments can be fairly well explained in
light of technical developments which occurred in our handcrafts. To
wit, cultural innovations in Japan have always been applied first and
most extensively in the area of our matsuri. I think that there is a
very complicated social psychology working in this; at any rate, due
to such developments sairei were established as a unifying point and
source of supplication in many castle towns and port cities. At the

same time, however, such <u>matsuri</u> came to be very different from what
they had been in earlier times. This is an additional reason for
establishing an opposition between <u>sairei</u> and the many other kinds of
<u>matsuri</u>.

v

What was the one most important change in the history of mat-
<u>suri</u>? In a word, it was the growth of crowds of what we might call
"spectators." It was the appearance among the participants in a
<u>matsuri</u> of people who did not share their beliefs and who could be
said to observe the rituals occurring during a <u>matsuri</u> merely in
order to appreciate their splendor. While the emergence of such
spectators brightened up city life and enlivens our childhood memories, it also slowly destroyed the unity of the beliefs which had
been centered about the shrine. In the end it fostered the tone of
thought that a <u>matsuri</u> is something to watch, even for those living
in the community in which it is performed. Without doubt this is not
a new attitude for it had already seeped into rural life before the
Meiji Period. Japan's farming population has always been inclined to
carry out a "<u>matsuri</u> worth watching"[19] during the years in which
their village economy was prosperous. They also have never done away
with their traditional sensitivities, and their desire to periodi-
cally renew the bond between the gods and their ancestors has gone
unchanged. Due to these factors, many amalgamations of old and new
rituals have occurred. Starting with the largest scale <u>sairei</u>,
countless gradations of <u>matsuri</u> have come into being, so many that it
is almost impossible to generalize all of them under one term. "Mat-
<u>suri</u>," accordingly has come to include many diverse rituals. Among
these, an especially complex one--one whose development is somewhat
difficult to understand by merely observing different instances of
it--concerns the procedure for receiving the gods in the <u>matsuri</u>

19.　<u>mirareru matsuri</u>　見られる祭

area. Several years ago I arrived in Ontake in Kōshū on the day of the summer sairei and, as a traveler, had the honor of observing it in detail. In this matsuri, following the appearance of a portable shrine, there was a ritual in which a priest, holding a mirror with his sleeves, presented it from the inner sanctuary of the shrine and placed it inside the portable shrine. There was also, however, a sacred horse in the middle of the procession. I was told that this horse had been borrowed from a supporting family in the village. It was not, however, for the priest to ride; nor was it merely led as a decoration. It had a special saddle in the middle of which stood a gohei.[20]

The curious thing about this gohei was that at each matsuri every year strips cut from white paper were wrapped around its shaft one after another, so that it was taking on a remarkable shape, like that of a perfectly round top. There is no doubt but that this was originally meant to be a "seat" for the gods. This means that even though a new, decorated portable shrine had been in use for some time, its introduction never necessitated abandoning the much earlier practice of receiving the gods with a sacred horse: the two vehicles simply came to be used together.

While at this shrine the earlier form of divine "seat" used during a matsuri was a gohei or a mitegura,[21] there have also been shrines at which people were used. It is not unusual even today to find cases in which, after a deity is respectfully bid to enter such a person, he or she is carried or placed on horseback and taken to the matsuri grounds. Many "hitotsumono"[22] were this kind of divine

---

20. 御幣 . A pole or stick which frequently has paper or cloth strips fastened to one end.

21. ミテグラ . In its current usage this term is largely synonymous with "gohei." See previous note.

22. ヒトツモノ . This refers to the "seat" of a deity. This frequently is a child who often appears on horseback in the processions of matsuri. The child usually wears elaborate clothing and headgear and frequently has a mark painted on his or her forehead.

"seat." There are also, however, places like the Shingū shrine in
Kumano at which a doll on horseback has been, for no one knows how
long the hitotsumono. In this case, stuck in the waist of the doll,
or attached to the edge of its hat, is a kind of sacred plant through
which it is thought a deity enters the doll. Naturally, since this
is the most mysterious part of the event, those conducting the
matsuri usually do not want to show it to nonbelievers. There are
also some cases in which this is even referred to as "the matsuri of
darkness"[23] and at this point all of the houses of the community dim
their lights and the procession passes without being seen by anyone.
The frightening legend of the one wheeled wagon[24] also springs from
this. Another story, told on the Izu Islands during the "Time of
Imi"[25] or the Hiimisama Matsuri[26] on the twenty-fourth of the first
month, goes so far as to state that anyone seeing a sacred ship with
a red sail crossing the sea on this day will die. Since such customs
concerning the passage of the gods encourage as many people as
possible to worship, they must be viewed as marking a large transition in the nature of our matsuri. Although ardent believers feel
that the descent of the gods is the focal point of a matsuri and ad-
here to the admonition that it should not be witnessed by those who
do not possess certain qualifications,[27] those lining the roads during a matsuri, particularly the women and children, have generally

---

23. kurayamimatsuri 暗闇祭 .

24. katawaguruma 片輪車 .

25. Ki no Hi 忌の日 . This matsuri is characterized by a
very strict period of imi 忌 (ritual abstinence) during which people
must abstain from such things as making loud noises, leaving their
homes, or permitting others to enter them.

26. 日忌様 . This is also one of several names given the
deity, or accsording to some accounts the ghost, which is associated
with a ship crossing the sea during this period.

27. Such qualifications include criteria such as: ritual
purity, rank within one's household, community membership, and a
fixed rotation of duties.

paid little attention to this. Accordingly, the descent of the gods has lost its former significance and has become a spectacle. For example, in the early medieval literature describing the omatsuri at Kamo, people are depicted as constructing grandstands and pulling their ox carts to a stop and even climbing trees to wait expectantly for the procession to pass before them. Due to the "creative splendor"[28] of these processions not only have they become daytime events, but the matsuri day, which is thought to have originally been one continuous period, has been divided into two parts. Furthermore, the latter half of a matsuri is nowadays referred to as "the real matsuri,"[29] or "the real day"[30] or "the auspicious day."[31] I would now like to move on to a consideration of certain earlier practices.

vi

Many scholars now agree that in ancient times the day for the Japanese began at what we currently think of as being about six in the evening, or twilight. It is for this reason that the term "yesterday evening"[32] is still to be found throughout the country referring to what is more commonly called "the night before last."[33] In connection with this it should also be noted that the evening meal on the last day of the twelfth month is termed either "Passing into the New Year"[34] or "Acquiring a Year."[35] I feel that our matsuri days

---

28. See footnote 18.

29. honsai 本祭 .

30. tōjitsu 當日 .

31. hi no hare 日のはれ .

32. kinōno ban きのうのばん .

33. issakuban 一昨晩.

34. toshikoshi 年越し . A number of special observances are associated with this evening throughout the country.

35. toshitori 年取り . During this evening people and in some areas tools and domesticated animals are said to become a year older.

also used to have these boundaries. In other words, they began with
the evening offering of what currently we think of as yesterday and
were completed with the morning offering the following day. It also
seems that the noon meal used to be restricted to being exclusively
outdoors. Thus, this single nighttime period between twilight and
morning was the most important part of a matsuri. During it, matsuri
were for the most part conducted indoors with a bonfire burning nearby outside. It was natural, however, that many people came to interpret this ritual as continuing through two days, when they came to
feel that midnight was the end of one day and that a new day began
with the ascent of the morning sun and the dawning of the eastern
sky. This, once again, constitutes a large transition in the nature
of our matsuri. In spite of this, however, there are still many old
people who feel that the matsuri vigil is more important than the
following daytime ceremonies. Since they feel, however, that matsuri
continue for two days, they consider it proper to go to the shrine
twice. Thus it has become natural for them to go to the shrine once
in the evening, after which they return home, change their clothes,
and go to bed. On the following day they once again go to the
shrine. Expressions referring to all night vigils such as "oko-
mori"[36] or "sanrō"[37] are still to be found only in rural areas.
Since this constitutes a drastic change, we should be able to find
other traces of it in practices being continued today. For example,
there is some doubt as to whether words like "yoimiya"[38] and "yom-
iya"[39] did actually refer to a nighttime shrine visitation. From the
western Chūgoku area to Kyūshū, these terms are variously known as
"yodo,"[40] "the evening of the yodo,"[41] or "the night of the

---

36. 御籠 .

37. 参籠 .

38. 宵宮 .

39. 夜宮 .

40. ヨド .

41. yodonyoru ヨドン夜 .

yodo"[42] and there is also the term "visit the yodo."[43] Accordingly, since the beginning of a matsuri is referred to as "the establishment of the yodo"[44] and the end as "the withdrawal of the yodo,"[45] it is clear that the "yodo" refers to the purified building or structure within which matsuri are conducted. Correspondingly, the term "yoimiya" probably also refers to such places. If this is true, then one may once again conclude that the central rituals of our matsuri were originally contained in an indoor service, while "the auspicious day," chiefly done as a beautiful outdoor spectacle during the daytime, was originally a celebration following the completion of the matsuri, one which is thought to have belonged to those centered about the illumination of the eastern sky.[46] At least it seems one would not err in saying that while sairei have been chiefly daytime events, matsuri originally were carried out chiefly during the night.

This concentration of matsuri rituals in the evening is, if one searches, still widespread among the common people of Japan, and it also is clearly evident in the rituals of the Imperial Court. This may be seen in the yearly Harvest Matsuri[47] following the ripening of the autumn crop, in the sacred music and dancing which is performed near the end of the winter, and of course in the Great Thanksgiving

---

42. yodoban ヨド晩.

43. yodomairi ヨド参リ .

44. yodo o tateru ヨドを立てる.

45. yodoharai ヨド払い.

46. This is an apparent reference to feasts which started in the evening and continued until dawn.

47. niiname matsuri (also shinjōsai) 新嘗祭 . This matsuri is now offered by the Emperor to the Imperial ancestors in appreciation for the harvest. It is thought, however, to date from the introduction of rice agriculture in Japan and to have been widespread among the common people until the unification of the country under the Imperial Court.

Matsuri[48] following the enthronement of a new emperor. Such ceremonies are still attended by one representative chosen from every
group among our domestic officials as well as those sent to our
foreign territories. Following the evening offering at these rituals
everyone withdraws _en masse_ to the assembly hall for an all night
vigil and is given something to eat. Then when the dawning sun once
again illuminates the sky, everyone attends the morning offering.
These ancient and revered practices, however, are very difficult to
maintain in our current busy times. While the rituals of the Imperial household are a highly venerable matter, it is clear that the
time of their evening offerings has become much later and their
morning ceremonies are now begun before dawn. Thus the period between them is becoming very short. Although I will not go into
whether this is for the better or the worse, the _matsuri_ of Japan
were usually, in their older forms, all night observances continuing
from the evening offering to the morning offering, during which
everyone remained in purified clothing. It will suffice if I state
that in some districts, even now, this practice of shutting oneself
up in a shrine for a night, known as "_oyogomori_"[49] is still observed.
Although the term "_otsuya_"[50] which is found in urban areas refers to
an all night vigil, such vigils are now limited only to times of
death, a practice which is also found in some rural areas. Accordingly aside from wakes, all night rituals have all but disappeared
from our urban _matsuri_.

---

48. daijōsai 大嘗祭 . This is the first Harvest _Matsuri_
(see previous note) conducted by an Emperor following his
enthronement.

49. 御夜籠 .

50. 御通夜 .

vii

As we have seen, the sense and feeling of old words come to
change with the passage of time. In spite of this, if one reads
carefully, it is not difficult to become aware of the differences
between their old and modern usages. "Matsuri" as successive generations of scholars have explained, is the same as "matsurō."[51] If
said today, this could be expressed as "waiting upon,"[52] or possibly
as "serving."[53] More concretely, this is epitomized in that attitude
with which everyone senses the disposition of the gods; if they have
any desires everyone heeds them and strives to fully carry them out.
In former times this was by no means merely an expression of one's
respect from a distance. Even though at present the Japanese term
"to visit a shrine"[54] apparently includes even the act of briefly
stopping simply to remove one's hat and bow, it has not yet come to
include merely lowering one's head when passing a shrine in a bus or
train. The earlier meaning of this term in both Japanese and Chinese
referred to being present at a fixed place and staying there for at
least a certain period of time, as is expressed in the usage of
"presence"[55] or "participation."[56] When this term is used in jest it
is extremely discourteous, and implies an attitude of submissive
resignation. Another example--one which has rarely been noticed--is
that our bowing has, in general, become much more abrupt. Compared
with bowing, however, the changes in our shrine visitations have been

---

51. マツラフ （服ふ or順ふ). This term is generally viewed
as meaning "to obey" or "to submit."

52. osoba ni iru 御側に居る . This phrase refers to contexts where a servant or lower person "waits upon" his master or
lord.

53. hōshi 奉仕 .

54. mairu マヰル .

55. sanretsu 参列 .

56. sanka 参加 .

of a much more extensive nature. Although today even the most devout
people do not think that there is anything unusual in the manner in
which they stand and bow in front of the gods, their way of worshipping cannot be found in any pictures over one hundred years old. To
the contrary, in earlier times people sometimes even worshipped on
their knees with their fans spread before them. The current way of
visiting shrines probably sprang from practices which apparently
quickly became disorderly, known as "circuit pilgrimages"[57] or
"pilgrimages"[58] in which one made visitations to several shrines
while enroute to a certain one. At any rate, because of this, the
distance between _matsuri_ and shrine visitations has become even
greater, and as a result the latter have acquired the status of a new
ritual belief. This was by no means due merely to the influence of
foreign religions. At big shrines, even today, the term "formal
visitation"[59] is found, and although such visitations have become
rather simple, it is evident that they are organized by the shrine
and are "provisional _matsuri_."[60] In other words, it used to be that
"to visit a shrine"[61] was the same as "to confine oneself within a
shrine,"[62] both of which implied participation in certain rituals.
Accordingly, in earlier times, when one did not possess the qualifications necessary for serving in a _matsuri_, one could not have performed a shrine visitation. In that this relation between shrine
visitations and being confined in a shrine must be touched upon
again, I will not go into details here. But, if the world changes
and the conditions of life become different, then even a ceremony as
important as a _matsuri_ must also undergo changes. Consequently,

---

57. _junpai_ 巡拝 .

58. _junrei_ 巡礼 .

59. _seishiki sanpai_ 正式参拝 .

60. _rinjisai_ 臨時祭 .

61. _mairu_ 参る .

62. _komoru_ 籠る .

while on the one hand the interval between the evening and morning offerings has been greatly shortened, on the other, the overall period of a <u>matsuri</u> has been increased in that they now begin before and finish after they used to. Furthermore, the daytime outdoor festivities connected with <u>matsuri</u> have become more numerous and have come to be viewed as being important. These are the things which I see as constituting the transition from <u>matsuri</u> to <u>sairei</u>. Anyone who aspires to know the unchanging essentials which run through three thousand years of <u>matsuri</u> in Japan must first recognize these striking differences between periods. If there is, in the cities and the villages, in the southwest and the northeast, and in almost every district, one line to be discovered joining all of the extremely diverse appearances of <u>matsuri</u> throughout the country, then our first characterization of it could be as a path which leads back to the practices of our ancestors. That self-serving way of thinking which bases a hastily constructed idea upon a person's limited experience, and states both that a given matter must be formulated in a certain way and that any deviations from such a formulation must be inaccurate, is likely to miss even essential points. The current status of our knowledge about our own traditions is such that the loss resulting from such an approach effects us all.

viii

I am afraid I may have been somewhat verbose, but few disciplines in Japan have been troubled by the stubborn attitudes of scholars as much as have Shintō studies. In that newer studies have always been considered to be more authoritative than earlier ones, there has fortunately been no great amount of bickering among scholars. At the same time, however, during the three hundred years of the Edo period in which countless varieties of interpretations appeared no two of these were ever complementary, and an accumulative study was never produced. With the passage of years, such studies have not only become more irksome, but have also come to lack any sense of direction. This is due to the fact that no one has ever attempted thoroughly to collect and compare the facts. I should not go so far as to state categorically that no one has ever attempted this. Although people such as Ban Nobutomo[63] and Kurogawa Shunson[64] did follow such an approach, in recent years this kind of scholarship has all but disappeared. Nonetheless, there is a scholarship which tries to base itself upon the facts, instead of immediately responding that something is due to the ignorance of the people, or that someone is mistaken, inquires into whether there are such things and, if there are, continues to inquire into them until their origins are known. The time has come for such a research technique to be applied also to planning the future of our country.

In line with the above, we are taking a gradual approach to developing our understanding of Japan's matsuri. The conditions which must have brought about this shift from matsuri to sairei and from shrine confinement to simply visiting a shrine were not necessarily external to the realm of matsuri. On the contrary, it seems that there are also many cases in which such tendencies were foreshadowed in the early developments of matsuri themselves. If a tendency may also be viewed as a characteristic, then we have a means through which we might characterize the fundamental beliefs relating to matsuri even from the changes which they have undergone. For example, in some of the scenes of sairei mentioned earlier, large banners fluttered in the wind. If, as it became possible both to change such banner material from hemp to cotton, and to dye characters upon it in India ink, people also came to be able to read and write these characters, then it would only be natural that they would not want them to flutter too much in the wind, and would consequently attach loops along the length of one side through which a pole could

---

63. 伴 信友 (1775-1846). A leading scholar of the Kōshōgaku school of National Learning and a prolific writer.

64. 黒 川春村 (1799-1866). A scholar of the same school as Ban Nobutomo. His interests ranged from the study of grammar to that of ancient art.

be passed. This full process reflects nothing other than the development of a desire to proclaim, at first only somewhat effectively, that a given place is the matsuri ground or that a matsuri is being conducted within a given house. It would not be mistaken to state that the simple erection of a pole as a marker of the matsuri ground is a characteristic feature of matsuri which dates almost from their inception. This practice is probably not limited to Japan, for if other people even half-heartedly believed that gods descent from the skies, they also would most likely erect such poles. This is because they serve as markers for the gods traveling in the skies. Since they are markers, during the day things which attract one's attention easily, for example, paper shide,[65] hemp thread, and different kinds of cloth would be attached to them. Because, however, these things can no longer be seen once it becomes dark, an attempt would always be made to light a fire. Raising a fire to the top of a tall pole used to be an extremely difficult feat. In areas which had rituals involving the standing of a pine tree, if there was a ceremony in which a great bonfire was lit, this ceremony would always be accompanied by a torch throwing competition. A basket containing fuel would be attached to the top of a pole and people would try to ignite it from below by throwing torches at it. (Reference to this may be found in my essay, "Thoughts on Pine Pillars.")[66] When convenient hanging lanterns and small garden lanterns became available, everyone used them. Subsequently when taller garden lanterns then became available, hanging lanterns came to be associated with sairei. The origin of the consecrated light[67] which has a very close relation with today's matsuri is very old and most likely also came into use under these conditions. Many old practices have also been passed

---

65. して . These are strips of folded white paper. They are seen as designating a sacred object or area.

66. Hashiramatsu-kō 柱松考 Teihon, volume 11.

67. otōmyō 御燈明 . These lights are burned at shrines throughout the period when offerings are placed before the gods.

down in the matsuri of the Imperial Court. During the nighttime portions of such matsuri light has traditionally been supplied by
torches or bonfires. At the Great Thanksgiving Matsuri which I attended following the enthronement of the new Emperor at the beginning
of the Taisho Period, however, there was a great deal of apprehension
about the danger of fire, and for the first time a portable electric
light, the bulb of which was shaped like a flame, was used. Although
electric lights seemed very much out of place when they first replaced the all-night lamps of village shrines, nowadays such things
are taken for granted and no one ever becomes concerned with them.
It seems that when matsuri used to be conducted on evenings when
there was no full moon they were relegated to being events which
could be seen only poorly. In the cities, however, it used to be
that in an effort to make these into beautiful "matsuri worth watching" an unbelievable number of candles were used. Compared with such
matsuri, those found in most villages seemed somewhat forlorn in that
aside from one's relatives, who were simply invited for a meal, no
spectators could be attracted. In some cases, however, villagers included a great deal of pageantry in their matsuri. Although such
pageantry was very poorly suited to their villages, it caused their
matsuri to become famous regional sairei. Such innovational sairei
are today still numerous particularly in the prefectures having ex-
ceptionally high populations near Kyōto. Large sairei are also occasionally found near the sea and in prosperous agricultural villages.
In some villages people boast of legends of unknown origin in which
it is related that their guardian deity enjoys very animated, noisy
affairs. Although they always state that things have been the way
they now are since the distant past, in fact, such practices have
only gradually come into being in recent years. Those people who
have lost touch with their traditions have through the years been
able to change the general conception of a matsuri and people have
come to feel that the small village matsuri which have no particular
attractions are little more than nuisances.

ix

Even though the link between _matsuri_ and city culture is fairly pervasive, the seasonal nature of _matsuri_ remains clear to everyone. According to my recollections, city _matsuri_ are particularly numerous during the summer. There were, however, few summer _matsuri_ in ancient times. Although there were probably occasions when _matsuri_ were held at the change of each season, the largest _matsuri_ of the year used to be those which, following the fall harvest, were conducted at a time when people were rich in products. Next in size were those which were conducted by farming villages towards the end of spring or early in the summer just before the preparation of the rice nursery began. It seems that the eighth of the fourth lunar month has traditionally been closely associated with mountain _matsuri_.[68] It is furthermore nearly certain that, as is often stated, the spring and autumn _matsuri_ mark the beginning and the end of the agricultural and particularly the rice cultivation period. This is because on certain days preceding and following this period, when the mountain gods descend to the rice paddies, and when the rice paddy gods enter the mountains, _matsuri_ are held for them in many villages. In some areas these _matsuri_ are attributed to the deity _Ebisu_[69] going to work on one of these days while the deity _Daikoku_[70] is said to return from work on the other. Nonetheless, I think that the original idea is the same as that on which the National Harvest _Matsuri_ during

---

68. This is the Buddha's birthday. One of the many practices which are associated with this day throughout Japan involves attaching flowers to the end of a long bamboo pole and then erecting it in one's garden.

69. えびす様. This popular deity is one of the Seven Deities of Good Fortune. Although it is thought that the belief in him originally developed within fishing communities, he is now associated with commercial and agricultural concerns also.

70. 大黒様. This deity is often associated with Ebisu and is another of the Seven Deities of Good Fortune. Beliefs related to him have evolved in a complicated manner and can be traced back to China and India.

the fall and the <u>Toshigoi Matsuri</u>[71] during the second lunar month are based.

It is thought that calendars were first produced in Japan in order to clarify both the agricultural year and the dates of <u>matsuri</u>. For certain, originally there were no regular festivities of any nature which were not in some way related to <u>matsuri</u>. Among samurai households, the "five festive occasions"[72] used to be stressed, but among farmers, the major "seasonal festivities"[73] were on the third of the third month and the fifth of the fifth month. Although they did not consider New Year's and the seventh of the seventh as normal days, many people did not go so far as to include these among their regular seasonal festivities. There are also areas in which the ninth day of the ninth month was viewed as a seasonal festivity. This particular day, however, was greeted with a somewhat different feeling. In many areas on this day large <u>matsuri</u> or <u>sairei</u> have traditionally been conducted. For example, in the northern half of Kyushu, "<u>kunchi</u>"[74] refers to the day of the village shrine's annual autumn <u>matsuri</u>. While this is written in characters either as "day of offerings"[75] or "shrine day,"[76] it originally came from "<u>kunichi</u>"

---

71. 祈年祭 (also <u>kinensai</u>). This <u>matsuri</u> is traditionally held on the fourth of the second lunar month. It is performed by the imperial household for an abundant harvest and the prosperity of the land.

72. <u>gosekku</u> 五節供 . These were standardized during the Tang period in China and came to be widely observed among samurai households in Japan during the Tokugawa Period. They traditionally include: New Year's, the third of the third month (Doll's Festival), the fifth of the fifth month (Boy's Festival), the seventh of the seventh month (The Star Festival), and the ninth of the ninth month (Chrysanthemum Festival). For a detailed discussion of these see U. A. Casal, <u>The Five Sacred Festivals of Ancient Japan</u> (Tokyo, 1967).

73. <u>sekku</u> 節供 .

74. クンチ .

75. 供日 .

76. 宮日 .

(the ninth).[77] Since, however, there are some areas in which <u>matsuri</u> are not conducted on the ninth of the ninth month, people have come to feel that "<u>kunchi</u>" does not refer to the ninth. There were many villages, including my own[78] which in order to extend the happiness of the fall <u>matsuri</u> and the mutual visiting in the neighborhood purposefully lengthened the period of this <u>matsuri</u> so that it would occur not only on the ninth of the ninth month, but also on the eighth or the tenth and sometimes the eleventh. At about the end of the Meiji period, however, the disadvantages of not having a uniform <u>matsuri</u> day were recognized and it was fixed on the ninth. In various parts of the Kantō area the word "kunichi"[79] is also found. Although this is clearly viewed as referring to the ninth of the ninth month, depending on the ripeness of the crop, the term "the three ninth's"[80] is also sometimes used, meaning that the <u>matsuri</u> day could fall on the ninth, the nineteenth or the twenty-ninth of this month. Although there are probably exceptions to this, it seems that in the Kantō area grand <u>matsuri</u>, which could even be termed <u>sairei</u>, are carried out during the spring with the ninth of the ninth month merely a day for a quiet "Eating <u>Matsuri</u>"[81] carried out in individual homes. During this day people enjoy themselves by visiting relatives and drinking <u>sake</u>. Even though it is a very quiet day, banners are erected in riding grounds and drums are beaten at shrines, and, in western Japan, it is referred to as a "<u>Tōyamatsuri</u>."[82] At such

---

77. 九 日 . The standard pronunciation for this term is "kokonoka."

78. Yanagita Kunio was born during the evening of July 31, 1875 in the Tsujikawa section of the village of Tawara Kantō county, Hyōgo Prefecture. This village is currently known by the name of Fukuzakichō.

79. ク ニ チ .

80. mikunichi 三 九 日 .

81. kuisai 食 ひ 祭 .

82. 頭 屋 祭 "Tōya" refers to a member of a community who is chosen, as its representative, to undergo a period of ritual abstinence (<u>imi</u>) and conduct a <u>matsuri</u>.

matsuri there are none of the attractions and processions which characterize sairei, and accordingly, there are no crowds of spectators. Quite to the contrary, they seem to approach what we imagine matsuri to have been like prior to medieval times.

Aside from the spring and fall matsuri, the winter ones are also very old. They are, however, in a state of decline in urban areas. Just as in medieval Christianity, Christmas denoted the return of spring, so also does the winter solstice of the Chinese calendar. These both refer to the day on which the sun becomes weak; a time which in Japan is usually characterized by the kindling of a great bonfire in order to renew its strength. Although in the Kinki region such a bonfire is the central feature of a matsuri which is apparently associated with iron smiths known as "The Fire Kindling Matsuri,"[83] in certain villages it is known by names such as "The Divine Torch."[84] Those observances dealing with dancing and music at the Imperial Court which I mentioned earlier probably share a common origin with this matsuri. This is because in earlier times they were centered about the burning of a bonfire--even though music is now their central feature. Large fires are also burned in the mountain villages of Mikawa at both flower matsuri and dance performances. While such fires are also burned during the snow matsuri found in the mountains of southern Shinshū near Mikawa, in general, musical dances are now more numerous than rituals involving the use of bonfires. In any case, it seems that in cold areas, matsuri such as these were particularly stressed in order to accentuate the feeling that everyone was waiting for the spring to arrive.

X

While villages located in mountainous areas have many winter matsuri, those found in flatter regions have a greater number of

---

83. ohītaki 御火燒き.

84. saitō サイトウ.

summer _matsuri_. Such _matsuri_ are also plentiful in both large and
small urban areas and particularly in those regions lying near the
water, such as coastal villages and ports. Although I by no means
think that this situation developed merely in response to the demands
of the cities, it should be noted that the enjoyment of an evening
stays with one much longer in areas where lights from many homes are
reflected in a body of water. The necessity to conduct a _matsuri_
once again when the warmer months begin is probably found from even
earlier times, however, among agricultural communities. In Kyōto,
the unusually named god, _Gion_,[85] is the central figure of a _matsuri_
conducted during the sixth lunar month. Though in eastern Japan
people often speak of the god _Tennō_,[86] since _Gozu Tennō_[87] is an old
name for _Gion_, it would seem that all of these names refer to the
same god. At any rate, nowadays this god is generally associated
with the Yasaka Shrines. A fairly large number of such shrines have
branched off from the one dedicated to the deity _Tennō_ at Tsushima in
Owari. There are, however, many differences in belief between two
Tennō shrines. For example, whereas there are eight "child Deities"[88] at the _Tennō_ shrine in Hachioji, there is only one minor
deity known as _Yagorōsan_[89] at the _Tennō_ Shrine in Tsushima. It also

---

85. 祇園 . This deity is now enshrined throughout Japan.
The shrine dedicated to _Gion_ in Kyōto was erected in the middle of
the ninth century.

86. 天王さま .

87. 牛頭天王 .

88. mikogami 御子神 . Since this name appears in the
Engishiki 延喜式 (compiled 927 A.D.) the belief in such deities is
felt to be very ancient. These "child deities" are closely related
to both the ancestral gods and to a variety of other beliefs in
different areas. In addition, pairs of mother-child deities are
found enshrined throughout the country. The child is usually a son
and often appears in folk literature.

89. 弥五郎 . In certain areas misfortune or evil is transferred to straw dolls known as "_yagorō_" which are then thrown away or
burned.

seems that there are Tennō Shrines where neither of these practices
is found and that there are areas in which observances of various
matsuri, among them the Tennō Oroshi Matsuri,[90] differ. Nonetheless,
a common feature shared by all of the Tennō Shrines is that their
matsuri days traditionally have been on the first, the seventh, and
the fourteenth or fifteenth of the sixth month. These days are also
matsuri days in areas in which there are neither Tennō nor Gion
Shrines. For example, in the San-In region the first day of the
sixth month traditionally has been referred to as "The day of
Renge"[91] and special foods like amigasayaki[92] have been prepared.
Also, throughout large areas of southern Kyushu matsuri known as
"Kawamatsuri"[93] are generally performed on this day at those places
where people obtain water. On this day various stories have traditionally been told about kappa[94] attacking blind female minstrels or
exchanging baby turtles. Accordingly this has been a day on which
people have cautiously approached bodies of water. Another example
concerns what I consider to be the highly unusual practices connected
with abstinence from cucumbers. These are detailed in A Glossary of
Seasonal Practices,[95] so I will be very brief here. In some areas

---

90. 天王おろし祭 .

91. renge no hi レンゲの日 .

92. 饂飩笠焼 . This refers to an offering made from the
flour of a popular form of noodle (udon). This flour is kneaded and
fried and then placed before the gods.

93. カハ祭. "Kawa" is a homonym of the Japanese term for
"river." It should be noted, however, that these matsuri are not
limited to bodies of flowing water but are also performed at ponds
and wells.

94. 河童 . These are malevolent water deities which often
appear in legends. They are thought to be strong amphibious creatures roughly the same size and shape as young children but with the
features of tigers, frogs, and birds. See U. A. Casal, "The Kappa,"
Transactions of the Asiatic Society of Japan, Third Series, volume 8:
157-199.

95. Saijishūzoku Goi 「歳時習俗語彙」by Yanagita Kunio.
The introduction is included in Teihon, volume 13.

following this day cucumbers are not to be eaten for a certain period, while in others on this day[96] or for a certain period leading up to it, they may not be eaten. A related practice involves writing the month and year of one's birth on a cucumber and then either placing it in a river so that it will drift downstream with the current, or offering it to the gods.[97] Even connected with the Gion belief in Kyoto there is a practice concerning cucumbers which is referred to as "gomonuri"[98] or "uryuishi."[99] If we cannot attribute all of these practices involving cucumbers to the dispersion of the belief in _Gion_, then this facet of the _Gion_ belief itself must have flourished due to a general folk belief concerning cucumbers.

It must have frequently been necessary for a rice-growing people to seek the favors of the water gods. Farmers not only recognized the benefits which could be gained from water, but were also well acquainted with the terror it could cause. Thus, while praying for one they would also pray to avoid the other. Whereas city inhabitants naturally did not raise rice and would therefore be less inclined to be thankful for the blessings of water, they were even better acquainted with the fearful nature of the damage it could cause. Consequently while in the country summer monsoons would be happily welcomed, in urban areas they were feared. During the Heian Period there were several dreadful epidemics which people felt shared

---

96. In the _Teihon_ edition the phrase "this day" is used, while in the _Kadokawa_ edition "this month" is used.

97. Various erotic tales are connected with this practice. For example, Shigeo Miyao in _Shokoku Sairei Angya_ (Tokyo, 1966) relates that a mischievous girl once, instead of offering such a cucumber to the water deities or _kappa_, first used it to "satisfy herself" and then offered it to them as if everything were normal. Due to her offense, the next time she was bathing in the river a _kappa_ snatched away "the testicles inside her anus" and from that time on drowned women have floated with their buttocks up because they were lighter than those of men.

98. 御紋瓜 .

99. 瓜生石 .

a common origin with monsoons and their resulting flooding. Though
these epidemics were also related to the rapid growth of cities, because they generally occurred during the summer, as did monsoons,
they both were apparently closely linked to the origin of our summer
matsuri. At any rate, developments which support this view appear in
the records of that time. The belief in spirits at this time did not
center about pacifying minor, easily angered spirits, but also involved praying to the deity Tenjin,[100] who was believed to possess
the strength to control not only these minor spirits, but also
natural calamities. Related matsuri known as "Goryōe"[101]and
"Shoryōe"[102] were not confined to the spirit halls of the upper Gion
and the lower Imamiya Shrines,[103] but were also conducted in both
Kitano and Otokoyama and were very popular. Many of these were
sairei held near the water during those summer months when it in-
flicted a great deal of damage. This leads one to imagine that
although water occupied a fundamental position in the lives of the
farmers, it was only after they began to live in large groups in the

---

100. 天神さま . Tenjin is one of the names under which
Sugawara Michizane (845-903) has been deified. He was an Imperial
advisor who worked to increase the power of the Emperor at the ex-
pense of the Fujiwara family. He was unjustly exiled to Kyushu in
901 A.D. where he died two years later. Shortly after his death
several of the people who had plotted against him died in quick suc-
cession. In that the goryō belief concerning avenging spirits (see
footnote 101) was widely held at this time, the court took various
steps, including the construction of the Tenjin Shrine in Kyoto, in
order to appease his spirit. During his life Michizane was a noted
scholar and is today, under the name of Tenjin, known as the god of
scholarship.

101. 御霊会 . This could be translated as "Spirit Matsuri."

102. 聖霊会 . This matsuri is performed as a memorial service for Shōtoku Taishi (572-621), one of the best known early em-
perors. He is credited with having played an important role in both
the development of Japan's relations with China and the propagation
of Buddhism in Japan.

103. The "upper" and "lower" used here indicate such shrines
are associated with a second shrine. One is frequently found on a
mountain while the other is located within a community.

cities that they quickly and unexpectedly experienced that flooding could introduce epidemics. There are, however, some shrines at which there are summer matsuri, but which do not belong to the groups of shrines mentioned earlier. For example, the gods of the Sumiyoshi Shrine[104] are old, as are the dispersed shrines to Ebisu. Even though it seems these gods were not petitioned to repel disease, their matsuri grounds are also found near the water among groups whose livelihood was based on commerce and transportation in which water played a vital role. Whereas the origin of summer matsuri lies in a common belief shared between city and farming peoples, it can be said that it was due completely to the strength of our city culture following the medieval period that summer matsuri became numerous in the manner that I mentioned, and that the matsuri of many areas became transformed into sairei.

---

104. 住吉の神 sumiyoshi no kami (also suminoe no kami). This is a reference to the three deities of the Sumiyoshi Shrine in Osaka. They are known as Uwazutsunoonomikoto 表筒男命 Nakazutsunoonomikoto 中筒男命 and Sokozutsunoonomikoto 底筒男命 . They were born when Izanaginomikoto 伊弉諾命 one of the two deities who created Japan, underwent a purificatory bath (misogi) after leaving the land of the dead. They are both the protector deities of those who travel on the seas, and the deities of harbors and also of poetry.

CONTRIBUTORS

BERNARD BERNIER is Professor of Anthropology at the University of Montreal. He has done field work in a rural community in Japan, and written Breaking the Cosmic Circle: Religion in a Japanese Village, Cornell East Asian Papers, #5.

J. VICTOR KOSCHMANN is Assistant Professor of History at Cornell University. He has edited and contributed to Authority and the Individual in Japan: Citizen Protest in Historical Perspective and (with Tetsuo Najita) Conflict in Modern Japanese History: The Neglected Tradition. He is interested in thought and action in modern Japanese history.

ŌIWA KEIBŌ is a Ph.D. candidate in the Department of Anthropology of Cornell University, and a graduate of McGill University, Montreal.

RONALD A. MORSE is Secretary of the East Asia Program, Woodrow Wilson International Center for Scholars, Smithsonian Institution, Washington, D.C. He has written "The Search for Japan's National Character and Distinctiveness: Yanagita Kunio (1875-1962) and the Folklore Movement," Ph.D. dissertation, Princeton; and translated The Legends of Tōno, by Yanagita.

STEPHEN NUSSBAUM is Assistant Professor of Anthropology at Earlham College and a Ph.D. candidate in the Department of Anthropology of Cornell University. His dissertation, based on research conducted in a "new town" in suburban Tokyo, deals with the creation of community in postwar Japan.

TADA MICHITARŌ is Professor at Kyoto University, Japan, and Director of the Research Group for Modern Folkways (Gendai Fūzoku Kenkyūkai). As a sociologist, essayist, and literary critic, he has published a number of books on Japanese popular culture. He has also introduced to Japanese readers the works of such contemporary French intellectuals as Roger Caillois and Jean-Paul Sartre. He gave a course on "La Sensibilite Japonaise" at the University of Montreal in 1982.

YAMASHITA SHINJI is Associate Professor at Hiroshima University, Japan. He has done field work in Tana Toraja, Indonesia, and is concerned primarily with death ritual, and the anthropology of performance and everyday life. He has published widely in Japanese anthropological journals, and from 1982 to 1984 was visiting fellow at the Department of Anthropology and the Southeast Asia Program, Cornell University.

YONEYAMA TOSHINAO is Professor of Anthropology at Kyoto University and the National Museum of Ethnology, Japan. He has done field work not only in Japan but in Tanzania and Zaire. His major interest in Japan is urban festivals such as the Gion Matsuri in Kyoto. He has written a number of books and articles, and organized a major symposium, on Yanagita Kunio. He taught anthropology at McGill University in 1981 and 1982.

CORNELL EAST ASIA SERIES

For ordering information, please contact Cornell East Asia Series, East Asia Program, Cornell University, 140 Uris Hall, Ithaca, NY 14853-7601, USA; (607) 255-6222.

8-93/.5M/BB